Praise for *When Cops Kill*

"As a thirty-five-year veteran police officer, I am often asked for my advice. My advice now is that every law enforcement officer should read this book!

"*When Cops Kill* covers both the human as well as the legal side of a critical incident. . . . Any law enforcement supervisor who cares about the officers under his or her command should want to read this book."

—Corporal Robert (Bob) Littler
Cobb County Police (Retired)

"LoRusso clearly understands the vernacular of the police rank and file because—besides being a top-notch lawyer representing officers and their unions—he is himself a cop. From the experiences of many of his law enforcement friends and clients, Lance is able to distill and accurately describe the psychological and emotional forces that are at play and that can prevent an officer from providing the most accurate account of the incident in the hours immediately following a critical incident. He suggests realistic and meaningful safeguards that will allow such incidents to be thoroughly and objectively investigated, while allowing the officer sufficient time to psychologically process the events and permit the post-incident effects of adrenaline overload to recede in order to provide an accurate account of the incident.

". . . Law enforcement administrators who read this book will find information that is invaluable to them in crafting agency policies, practices procedures, and training that ensure both justice and fairness to all involved in critical incidents. I am recommending *When Cops Kill* to all of my law enforcement command college students."

—Mike Caldwell, Esq.

"When Cops Kill is the most comprehensive review of law enforcement critical incidents and the events that follow for both the officer involved and the agency. With the current events occurring in law enforcement across our country, it is a must-read for both the street officer and the law enforcement administrator. Lance draws on his experience as both a cop and a lawyer in walking you through critical incidents and their aftermath. I highly recommend this book for all law enforcement officers, regardless of your rank or position."

—Ron Replogle
Law Enforcement Officer (Retired)

"As the wife of a policeman, this was very interesting information. Very useful in being prepared for situations my husband could potentially encounter in his job. I can be [of] better support to him with this knowledge."

—Deana Cole
Spouse of Law Enforcement Officer

"As a former police officer and current attorney, Lance brings a unique perspective to this important and timely issue. The advice given for police officers involved in a shooting is spot on. Lance's advice is also important for law enforcement leaders. The immediate decisions made by leaders of a department which has an officer-involved shooting can make or break the outcome—in some cases for both the officer involved and the department, if not handled correctly. This book is definitely as must-read."

—Billy Grogan
Senior Police Administrator

"Coming from someone who has been in a deadly force incident during law enforcement, I can say this was a great read and the information is true to the topic. I only wish I had read it before my incident, but it was still helpful after the fact. . . . This should be required reading for all police officers. I also hope as many family and friends of police read it, as well. It can benefit all of us in or around the police community."

—David Canup
Law Enforcement Officer

"*When Cops Kill* is a must-read for every police and law enforcement officer. The book contains a wealth of information that every officer needs to know, but is never taught in the academy. . . . As an investigator who works officer-involved shootings, I often see officers who are involved in critical incidents and who are not mentally prepared for the aftermath. From one officer to another, I highly recommend reading this book before you find yourself in one of these situations. I will be recommending this book to every officer in my agency."

—Johnnie Moeller
Police Investigator

WHEN COPS KILL

WHEN COPS KILL

The Aftermath of a Critical Incident

Lance J. LoRusso, Esq.

*BOOK*LOGIX®
Alpharetta, Georgia

ISBN: 978-1-61005-293-1

Library of Congress Control Number: 2012922798

10 9 8 7 6 5 4 3 2   0 8 2 2 1 7

Printed in the United States of America

∞This paper meets the requirements of ANSI/NISO Z39.48-1992 (Permanence of Paper)

The contents of this book are neither intended to, nor constitute legal advice. As always, you should consult an attorney with any specific legal issues or questions.

TASER® is a registered trademark of TASER International

Lance J. LoRusso, Esq.

Author of *Blue Line Lawyer,*
The Legal Blog for Cops

A Blue Line Lawyer publication

www.bluelinelawyer.com

DEDICATION

As people travel the world to fill their minds and hearts with memories, so too hearts and memories of law enforcement officers (LEOs) are filled during their journeys. The traveler experiences images and impressions of beauty and wonder sought out by choice and deliberation. The LEO involuntarily receives images and impressions of the worst side and sights of humanity. The commonality between the world traveler and the career LEO is that the sights, sounds and memories both gain will endure forever and shape their very souls.

This book is dedicated to the law enforcement officers who lost their lives in the pursuit of a belief that only through the law can society be preserved. For them, there is no end of watch; heroes never die. We all continue to serve with the memories of our fallen brothers and sisters close to our hearts until we meet them again.

I send my thanks and appreciation to the law enforcement officers who provided their stories and perspectives for this book. We receive them as testimonials to courage and further evidence of your dedication to the profession.

To my wife Barbara, who kissed me goodbye every day that I left the house in uniform never knowing if I would come home but never complained. Like the spouse of every law enforcement officer, she knew I was called to this profession. She is my driving force and an indescribable source of strength.

–Lance J. LoRusso

DISCLAIMER

What you will read in these pages will hopefully help you as a LEO. That is my sincere hope and sole intent. While you will read about scenarios, cases, case law, statutes, and outcomes, nothing in this book should be construed or is intended to provide legal advice to anyone in a particular situation. Consultation with an attorney, especially with regard to a critical incident, is a private, detailed, and time consuming process that requires, at a minimum, an exchange of information. As the delivery of information in this book is a one-sided process, it would be impossible for me to provide proper advice to anyone in a specific set of circumstances without a personal consultation.

In many instances, Georgia law will be used to illustrate examples. I will also occasionally cite the Model Penal Code. The Model Penal Code is an academic compilation of criminal codes that is used as a guideline for criminal statutes in many states. It was first published by the American Law Institute[1] in 1962 and updated in 1981. While no state has adopted the Model Penal Code *verbatim*, many states use the Model Penal Code as a foundation for current statutes. However, the principles of use of force and defenses to criminal actions are nearly universal throughout the United States. For example, the use of deadly force to stop a fleeing felon is governed by state law and guided by the United States Supreme Court decision of *Tennessee v. Garner*[2]. You should consult the law in your state, both statutory and case law, for clarification

---

[1] www.ali.org
[2] 471 U.S. 1 (1985)

and seek legal counsel with any questions or concerns that relate to a specific situation or issue. Finally, the case law cited in this book, like any case law, can be overruled, set aside or rendered meaningless by actions of a legislature or Congress. The law evolves and you must stay abreast of any changes.

CONTENTS

FOREWORD

All of my adult life, in one way or the other, I have been involved in law enforcement, or "chasing bad guys" as I like to say. I began at age nineteen when I joined my first branch of the military, the United States Coast Guard. Later on, I affiliated with the United States Air Force and was accepted into the United States Army 11ᵗʰ Special Forces, but never joined due to a bonus issue. I retired as a United States Navy Master at Arms Chief. Most of this time was spent as a Reservist.

In my civilian life, I joined the Cobb County Police Department at age twenty-two as a patrol officer. I served in all ranks and retired as a Deputy Chief. I hated retirement, so I went to work for the State of Georgia as an Investigator with the Georgia Peace Officer Standards and Training Council (POST). I didn't care about the big titles because I had the most fun as a young Detective or Detective Sergeant. Seven years later, I am still there trying to make a difference. The most disturbing part of my current position is when an individual tries to start a career in law enforcement and lies on the POST application. We do not need people like this in a profession where integrity is everything. Next step, a felony charge. This will be covered in Chapter 8.

I became acquainted with the author when he was a patrol officer with the Cobb County Police Department. I was impressed from the first time I met him. I knew he would go far in life, but I had no idea as to his path. As time went on, it became more and more evident he would always have his heart centered in law enforcement. Then he enrolled in law school. I thought he would get his degree and become a chief at a major department or run for a political office like Solicitor General or District Attorney. I was wrong. He became a major advocate for all law enforcement. He has dedicated almost all of his practice to helping those of us in law enforcement when we find ourselves needing a brilliant attorney and good advice.

This book was written from a perspective that few authors have ever experienced. Lance has been there as a beat officer (offered Sergeant and turned it down), prosecutor, and counselor. As the saying goes, "he has been there and done that!"

When I look back at my own career, there were many times I could have used the information contained in this book. This book should be mandatory reading for every law enforcement officer from agency head to recruit. This book is an easy read even though it is technical in content. It would have made my life much easier if it had been available in my time.

I have read every page and cannot find a single topic that I disagree with or on which I have a different take. I only wish I could be so eloquent. Thank you my friend. This book will help more officers than you will ever know.

–Tom Keheley
Deputy Chief, retired
Cobb County Police Department
Forty-two year veteran of law enforcement

Lance LoRusso has written a book that will help members of the law enforcement community deal with one of the hardest things that can happen to them during their careers.

The requirement to discharge your weapon in the preservation of life is never an easy decision and must be made in a split second, after which officers are subjected to intense investigations that question every decision he or she made. The investigation process is held during a period of time when an officer's emotions are at their most sensitive stage, and yet officers must endure armchair quarterbacks looking at very outcome and making a decision that will impact the rest of the officer's life.

This book gives officers an understanding of the process, as well as providing valuable tools to ensure that their rights are protected and that they are afforded as much due process as the law allows.

The subject of law enforcement involved shootings is not an easy subject to understand, especially when each and every case involves advocacy groups that support or harass the officers without sufficient facts to do so. This book provides a law enforcement perspective written by someone who has walked in our shoes. It is written from the heart, and provides officers with a detailed summary of what we can expect. I plan to recommend it to all law enforcement professionals as required reading.

– Chuck Canterbury
National President
Fraternal Order of Police
Twenty-Six Year Veteran of Law Enforcement

PREFACE

"Kill (v): To deprive of life; to destroy the life of an animal or person.[3]"

The word implies no malice or intent. It is a word describing an act or outcome. In the real world, when a LEO is forced to use deadly force to stop a forcible felony, apprehend a fleeing felon, or protect herself or another person, the outcome may be the death of the suspect. The subjective intent of the LEO is simply to survive the encounter, save the life of an innocent person and effect an arrest.

I worked as a street officer with the Cobb County Police Department in Georgia and as an Investigator with the Cobb County Solicitor's Office. I have also been sworn with the Cobb County Sheriff's Office since 1999 and was sworn with the Fulton County Sheriff's Office before I started with Cobb County Police. I have been involved in law enforcement continually since 1988. I have worked on the road as a patrol officer, public relations, investigations, trial support, training, and served on a hostage negotiation team. I have taught search and seizure, use of force, firearms, and legal issues at police academies since 1990. Through research and preparation for cases, classes, and this book, I have reviewed countless reports of officer involved shootings.

In 1999, I began my legal career when I graduated with honors from Georgia State University College of Law. I attended graduate school and law school at night while working. I am licensed to practice law in Georgia and Arkansas. I am admitted to all state and federal courts in

---

[3] Black's Law Dictionary 6th Ed.

the State of Georgia as well as the United States Supreme Court. Today, I represent LEOs. I am the General Counsel for the State Lodge of the Georgia Fraternal Order of Police and also serve as counsel for Local Lodge #13 of the Georgia Fraternal Order of Police, my home lodge. I teach classes on critical incident response and respond on a 24-hour basis to officer involved shootings and critical incidents. I have sat with officers when they gave statements, prayed, and cried. I stand up for you like you stand up for the strangers in your jurisdictions. As you will come to learn from these pages, I am prone to the occasional quip and humorous comment. Some of the funniest people I've ever met are LEOs so I find such comments completely appropriate in a book written for LEOs.

If you are reading this book, you are likely a law enforcement officer, the spouse of a law enforcement officer, or are working in law enforcement. So, I begin by thanking you for your public service. You know that a career in law enforcement is a family commitment. Missed birthday parties, anniversaries, and other family events take a toll, but that's okay. You do the job anyway. Low salaries, shift work, and miserable weather wear you down, but that's okay. You do the job anyway. Politics, what you see on the street, and dealing with the lower 2% of society's bell curve on a daily basis ratchets up the stress, but that's okay. You do the job anyway. Let's be honest, you got into the profession knowing you would face these issues.

This book is about the most stressful thing a LEO can possibly face: the taking of a human life. You know there is a risk of being forced to do this, but part of you believes you can probably get through a career and avoid it. This is especially true if you have no desire to work in a tactical unit or response team. Here's the reality: While you may indeed avoid it, you must prepare mentally for that potentiality.

This book is intended to help prepare you for that day. Make no mistake, I pray every night that you, and every officer, can avoid taking a life. However, my first prayer is that you come home safely. Sometimes one cannot occur without the other. Given the choice, I want you and every law enforcement officer home in one piece at the end of each shift.

I will use the term "law enforcement officer" or LEO throughout this book. I hope you will interpret this term to mean just that—ANYONE who puts on a badge and gun and agrees to be a part of that thin blue line that separates order from anarchy. Whether your badge says "police," "sheriff," "agent," "corrections," "trooper," "constable," "marshal," or any other law enforcement professional, we all share the same goal: to fulfill our sworn duties and return home at the end of each shift. Anyone who has ever been in a fight with a suspect knows that you do not care what the badge reads on the people who answer your call for backup. Much like jurisdiction, when you need help, your backup's title is the last thing on your mind and is just a minor detail for an incident report.

Through these pages, you will learn from firsthand accounts what it is like to be involved in an officer involved shooting. In some cases, the officer used deadly force and the suspect lived. In others, the suspect was killed by the officer or responding units. Still other situations involved a suspect who killed himself after the encounter with LEOs. In our ideal training scenarios, the officer shoots to stop the lethal threat and the suspect is disabled or dead. However, that is not the reality in every shooting. You will hear from LEOs who were shot. Some fired back and some did not. You will also hear from LEOs who were present when their partner was shot or used deadly force. Finally, you will hear from the spouse of a LEO about the night she got the call she feared every day he left the house in uniform. Only through these different perspectives can you see the many ways that the use of deadly force affects LEOs.

What really happens in LEO shootings? How many shots are usually fired? How far apart are the officer and the suspect? Here is where I draw the line in this book. I could fill this book with a truckload of statistics that would prove one thing—there are enough studies and statistics about LEOs to fill a train car. Critical incidents are not about statistics. They are about people.

I write this book with a unique perspective and focus. I will share this perspective with you in an effort to help you understand why I wrote this book. Wearing a badge, I have walked a mile in your shoes. As a lawyer, I advocate for officers involved in shootings from the street to the Grand Jury. I stand by LEOs—always have and always will. It is my hope that I can answer some of your questions, put some of your fears to rest, and help prepare you for the day we all hope never comes.

This book is not a textbook filled with scientific or social research. You can find plenty of those texts in any university criminal justice program written by very talented authors and researchers. Those resources provide valuable information you can use to supplement the information contained in this book, push for change within your agency, or pass legislation. I am not a researcher or professor. I am an advocate for LEOs.

I explore more fully here many topics that I address in my blog, www.bluelinelawyer.com. The blog is a great way for me to write on issues related to LEOs, comment on current events, and get the word out about recent case law. In several instances, I will include excerpts or entire articles from my blog. These articles constitute many hours of research. In all instances, the inclusion of prior printed materials from my blog is intended to enhance the reader's experience and relate a topic that raised my focus in the past. You may always read the complete article and current articles by visiting the blog. It is a blog for LEOs, and I welcome your suggestions and comments.

As you read this book, you will learn about communities that rose to support their LEOs in time of crisis, LEOs who came through horrific circumstances to live on in peace, and court decisions and legislative actions that reflect an appreciation for LEOs and the job that you do. Hopefully, this book will impart some sense of comfort that you will never serve alone.

I hope you enjoy the book, learn valuable information, and pass this information on to friends, family, and coworkers.

What happens to LEOs just before, during, and after a critical incident? How does the law handle the messy details of a fight for one's life or the taking of one life to save another? What are the civil ramifications of the use of deadly force? It is not enough to say, "You'll probably get sued if you use deadly force." What does that mean for the officer? What does that mean for the agency? Read on and let's learn together what happens...When Cops Kill.

–Lance J. LoRusso

ACKNOWLEDGMENTS

We all proceed through life with the help and influence of others. For better or worse, we are the sum total of our experiences. The concept of a sum implicitly involves positives and negatives that result in the total. I am extremely fortunate and blessed in my life that the positives far outweigh the negatives. However, I learned a lot from the experiences on both sides of the balance sheet.

I would like to thank some people here who have been positive influences in my life and contributed in one way or another to the writing of this book. Their contribution could have been in the form of encouragement generally or specifically related to this project. Some will wonder what they did specifically to appear on this list. However, that is not important. Some will appear with a reference and others will appear in name only. I thank them for taking some time to add to the richness of my life. Without the positive influences in my life, this book would not have been possible.

Robert J. Littler, my FTO for keeping me alive and supporting my love of law enforcement.

Robert E. Hightower for his constant mentoring, leadership and guidance. He continues to serve as a protector and warrior next to his Lord.

Tom Keheley for his guidance, friendship and consistent leadership by example.

Tony Wheeler for his friendship, patriotism and service to our country.

Tom Jones, Esq. and Joe Burford, Esq. for their constant encouragement and friendship.

Chuck Canterbury, National President of the Fraternal Order of Police, for his support, friendship and never forgetting what it is like to be a LEO on the street.

Joseph LoRusso, my dad for teaching me respect for LEOs from the time I could speak and listen.

Frank LoRusso, my brother for his constant support and unconditional love. My sister Maria for her support and encouragement.

Charles R. "Mike" Swanson, Phd. for keeping my dream to continue my education alive through his example.

George "Kirk" Kirkham for taking the challenge to see the real side of law enforcement and stretching his mind to change the face of LEOs throughout the United States.

All of the LEOs and spouses who patiently answered my questions during interviews.

The unofficial editors, Julie Wiedeman, Rebecca Sample, Esq., and Clay Strayhorn, Esq. People always remember the treasures of the pharaohs. They fail to recall the folks who had to dig through the sand in search of finding anything that was worth carrying in the hot sun. Thanks for digging.

CHAPTER ONE
BLESSED ARE THE PEACEMAKERS

Q: *I know you're a spiritual person. Did you consult your pastor?*

A: *My biggest controversy I had was spiritually because I had taken a life. I didn't know how to really deal with that so I called my pastor and asked him. He provided scripture for me, multiple scriptures which define murder and that murder is the sin and not the killing but the murdering. There's been righteous killing throughout the bible.*

– Twenty-three year veteran of law
enforcement

I like shooting, and I love hunting. But I never did enjoy killing anybody. It's my job. If I don't get those bastards, then they're gonna kill a lot of these kids dressed up like Marines. That's the way I look at it.

– Gunnery Sergeant Carlos Hathcock, II,
U.S.M.C.

Blessed are the peacemakers: for they shall be called the children of God.

– Matthew 5:9

Into the Deep End of the Pool

On July 10, 1990, I responded to a domestic dispute at an apartment complex in Marietta, Georgia. The complex was not the best, and my beat partner John Munro and I were definitely on alert. We both knew that anything could happen in a domestic dispute, but this complex was always different. The complex was known to contain overpopulated apartments, drug dealing was constant and LEOs could quickly find themselves outnumbered by unfriendly "observers." While this was the kind of call answered by law enforcement officers all the time, our concern that this call could be a bad one was the kind of feeling law enforcement officers experience every day. It was the type of sixth sense that keeps LEOs alive and they ignore at their own risk.

When we arrived, it seemed like every resident was in the parking lot. The place was a madhouse. It was morning watch, why were all these people outside after midnight? While I certainly had seen this behavior before, I noticed something strange about this crowd. They were overflowing with two emotions: fear and anger. As usual, we were the center of attention from the time we arrived. This was especially true when a woman came forward and told us that her boyfriend was inside the apartment holding her three-year-old son hostage.

The door was locked and we got the perpetrator to unlock the door. He did so quickly and then ran back to a deep upholstered chair in the living room of the apartment. When we pushed the door open, we saw this guy sitting in the chair with a little boy on his lap. In his right hand, he held a butcher knife up to the child's throat. John and I moved as far apart as possible and John tried to distract him so I could draw my weapon. At the time, I was shooting in a lot of competitions. I felt confident that I could shoot him in the face and end this stand-off quickly. When I moved to unholster my weapon, he pulled the knife up higher just under the child's jaw. As an EMT, I knew the child's carotid artery and jugular vein were both vulnerable. Then the suspect informed us that he was a former police officer, he knew we would try to shoot him, and he could act quicker than we could. He was right. So began my first negotiation with a hostage taker.

Some forty minutes later, John and I walked out of that apartment alive. My Sergeant, Dan Thomas, carried that little boy to his mother without a scratch on his body[1]. The suspect left in handcuffs. I was unable to sleep for six months without thinking about what could have been — or what should have been.

As with any crisis, this experience helped shape my career and my life. Almost three years later to the day, Officer Robbie Ingram with my agency was shot and killed. He was twenty-four years old. His death, along with the shootings of two of my friends in 1999, led me to the place where I stand today. I sought more knowledge and more opportunities to serve. I sought to serve not only the community, but also my fellow officers. Throughout this journey, I learned a great deal about the law, the science, and the impact of critical incidents.

It just never gets easy to hear. In my city, my state, my country, or elsewhere, the news stories about law enforcement officers (LEOs) killed in the line of duty chill my blood and stop my heart. From traffic stops, to domestic disputes, to stand offs and active shooters, LEOs

---

[1] Deputies later took out a warrant for her when she drove away from the sentencing hearing with the little boy riding on the gas tank of her motorcycle.

give their lives far too often in defense of the innocent[2]. LEOs form the first response and the last line of defense.

Since the murder of Georgia State Trooper Chad LeCroy on December 27, 2010, I have received numerous emails from friends and LEOs that contain calls to action. Trooper LeCroy's murderer is a career criminal who shows no sign of stopping his criminal pursuits. People have asked me, "Why would he shoot a LEO? Was he afraid of going back to prison?" I am confident that he was not afraid of returning to prison. Given his treatment in the criminal justice system, he would have no reason to fear that result. The truth behind Trooper LeCroy's murder will likely remain unknown. Every LEO reading this knows that you will never really get the truth from a criminal. Looking for the truth in the words of a cop killer is a pointless exercise.

I will never forget the LEOs who put on their uniforms and go to work hours after a LEO's funeral. As always, you are all in my thoughts and prayers. For many LEOs, it is the focus on the mission that keeps them moving past such tragedies. For most, I suspect, it is our faith in God. Whatever the source of our strength, LEOs continue to rise to the challenge and remain true to their pledge to uphold the law.

What can we do to move forward following these tragedies? I encourage all LEOs to remain focused. Get involved. Rest assured that you are not alone. Visit websites devoted to LEOs to share your opinions and find kindred spirits. I enjoy www.officerresource.com, the National Fraternal Order Police (www.grandlodgefop.org)

---

[2] Although this book is about critical incidents, many LEOs lose their lives in motor vehicle collisions. This is a trend we must all work to change.

and Georgia FOP (www.georgiafop.org) websites, BLUtube (www.blutube.policeone.com), Law Enforcement Today (www.lawenforcementtoday.com), and others. Meet with your local, state, and national legislators. Keep them informed. Sponsor and support legislation. You will find support for your causes. For instance, Trooper LeCroy's murderer was placed on probation several times even after arrests for possession of a firearm in the commission of a felony and being a felon in possession of a firearm. The National Rifle Association (www.nrahq.org/law) has pressed for mandatory prison sentences for these crimes for years. The NRA is a friend and supporter of LEOs.

You have a valuable voice! In 2011 and 2012, the Georgia General Assembly passed a bill I drafted that prevents a person from receiving First Offender Status if they commit a felony against or injure a LEO. I wrote this bill after I represented a LEO who had her arm broken by a DUI suspect. The district attorney allowed this guy to plead guilty with no jail time, no fine, and First Offender Status. Throughout the legislative process, I found the legislators very receptive and supportive of LEOs. In fact, the bill passed unanimously. They understand and appreciate your role and the risks you take. Take comfort in that support. Remain steadfast in your conviction that your efforts are selfless. Your efforts change the lives of others.

Be strong and know that the public supports you. Find strength in the courage and strength of others, like the family of Trooper LeCroy, who greeted an endless line of visitors in the funeral home. I looked into the eyes of Trooper LeCroy's youngest son at the funeral home as he stood at attention wearing gray pants, a blue shirt, and

Georgia State Patrol collar insignia. His courage inspired me and it was an honor to meet him. I know he will one day understand what it means to be the son of a hero. In the interim, we will all work to prevent our LEO family from losing another warrior. The funeral of Trooper Chad LeCroy represents the funerals for LEOs all over our country. The names of the fallen change, but the hurt and the impact do not. The death of a LEO is always personal.

Recently, my wife and I were privileged to meet one of America's heroes. He was a LEO wounded in the line of duty. He was being treated by the professionals at the Shepherd Center in Atlanta. As we welcomed him and his family to Atlanta and embraced them during this difficult time, we learned that another LEO arrived at the Shepherd Center the same week. As expected, the outpouring of caring and assistance expanded to that LEO as well. The collective arms of law enforcement are big enough to wrap around any brother or sister in need.

Where does this energy and seemingly endless flow of resources come from? The money comes from the pockets of LEOs. The energy comes from an appreciation and an understanding of what it means to put yourself second and your commitment to your community first. I have met LEOs from all over the world and there seems to be a common bond among us. While critics of law enforcement believe it is some dubious, unwritten code, they could not be more wrong. The job of law enforcement differs little from state to state and town to town. The same is true of the motivation and commitment of LEOs. So it is not surprising that when one of our members falls down, there are hundreds there to help him or her stand again.

I am fortunate that my mentors in law enforcement taught me that we must look after each other and that when LEOs do not work well together, only the bad guys win. Following the visit to the Shepherd Center, I was so proud to be part of the LEO family. I was proud to know that our temporary Georgia resident heroes and their families slept with the comfort that they were[3] not alone.

It is not hard to make the case of how important LEOs are to our society and our country or how much the public supports you. I know it is hard to reconcile the bad things that happen to these good people in uniform. Some LEOs are able to continue in their career after seeing the craziness they experience daily and leave a funeral for a fallen brother or sister without a deep seated faith in God. Perhaps, but I do not know any. Only through divine intervention will LEOs finish their shifts. While not all will come home, we must believe in a higher purpose.

Remember the killed and wounded LEOs you know and read about. Through focusing on their lives and passing, you must focus on your survival. The decision matrix to use deadly force is not complicated and can be taught in a few hours. I know this because I have taught this information to hundreds of LEOs and civilians. However, the *commitment* to use deadly force in defense of yourself, a fellow LEO, or a stranger must come from within. This requires a lot of soul searching, prayer, and introspection. Learn from these pages. Recommit to honor your oath to uphold the law and stay alive while doing so. Your efforts toward defining these goals in the comfort of your home or at the training academy will pay dividends on the street in the form of decreased hesitation, decisive action, and safety.

---

[3] One of those who welcomed this young deputy was Georgia Attorney General Sam Olens. We are so thankful for his continued support of law enforcement.

You are charged to act pursuant to an oath to preserve order in our country and protect life. You pledge to step forward when others take two steps back, to run toward the threats to our society when others run away, and to place your very life at risk for strangers. Blessed are the peacemakers.

CHAPTER TWO
TIME ENOUGH TO LIVE

This is one of the problems, neither one of us remember exactly what happened next. I want to say he obviously pulled a gun out of his pocket and I'll go back. I remember my partner telling him to take his hand out of his pocket. I was standing at about a ninety degree angle away from him. My partner was face to face with him. The next thing that I know for a fact is seeing the bullet coming at me. I do not know if my partner got shot first. He doesn't know if I got shot first. Neither one of us have any recollection of the other person being shot. I know that I started to go down to one knee and I had drawn my weapon. At that point I was hit. You can see the bullet coming at you, and it hit me just below my left eye. I was either spun or turned to get away. I couldn't see a thing at that point. I stumbled a few feet. I'm assuming I was shot again in the back at that point. We don't know when I was shot in the back. We're assuming that I was shot again at that point because there was a large pool of blood right there as if I had stopped and possibly gone down again to one knee and hesitated for a moment.

– Name withheld

We are all familiar with the iconic image of the two gunfighters squaring off. The scene is set for the "reckoning" between the two dominant characters. The entire town seems to know that tempers have come to a head and the resolution is near. The opposing forces gather in the shops on either side of the street and wait silently for the resolution of the mounting tension. Most important is the throng of onlookers who watch from porches, windows, and rooftops, confident that these two men[4] will display more accuracy than sense. Last, but certainly not least, the sun is out.

Anyone who has ever been involved in law enforcement knows just how far this scene is from reality.

First, nearly 60 percent of assaults on LEOs occur in darkness or low light conditions between the hours of 6 p.m. and 6 a.m.[5] Second, the officer and the suspect are most often the only people in the area. Finally, except for the rare circumstance, there are no witnesses. These three issues present a problem inherent in all shootings. The public has no idea what the use of deadly force involves and the circumstances under which it occurs. While this is no surprise to the LEO readers, I hope the rest of you will take heed. This is critical because, in my experience, tension and uncertainty emerge when reality and perception diverge. In response to these unknowns, people such as attorneys, jurors, prosecutors, family members, and the media "fill in the blanks" to avoid admitting they do not know the reality. This reality gap often gives birth to the negative connotations associated with LEO

---

[4] No sexism intended. I've just never seen a gunfight in a movie between two women. Perhaps they have more sense than to engage in such activities.
[5] 2001-2010 FBI Summary of Law Enforcement Officers Killed or Assaulted Table 67.

shootings. Even worse, they may fill those gaps with what they believe to be true based upon what they have seen in movies and on television.

How could a person shoot someone and not be able to recall basic details such as what the person said, the distance between them, and how many shots were fired? This is the basic question that gives rise to so many misperceptions about an officer involved shooting (OIS). The average person has little, if any, idea what it is like to be placed under severe stress and react to a threat. The closest they will come is a car wreck, so let's start there.

In a car wreck, the time between a perceived threat and the impact is generally a fraction of a second. Many times, there is no perception of the threat. This was the case in a civil suit I handled on behalf of a LEO. A person driving a large sedan turned left across two lanes of traffic on a divided highway. The speed limit was forty-five miles per hour. It did not end well. She suffered a severe fracture to her leg and the LEO endured shoulder and hand surgery. Both were entrapped in their vehicles. During the lawsuit, as I will discuss later, I took the deposition of the at-fault driver.

> *Q: When did you first see the white police car with the black push bumper, blue lights on top, and fluorescent markings?*
> *A: When it hit me[6].*

We have all either been involved in or investigated a car wreck. After the wreck, the average person is shaking,

---

[6] This is a near exact quote from the case.

confused, unable to stop talking, and amazingly uncertain of what occurred. "The car came out of nowhere," "all of a sudden the car was on top of me," "there was no time to react," "I had no time to think," and my personal favorite, "is that the car that I hit over there?" They are often unable to describe the color of a traffic light, the number of lanes on a roadway they travel on a daily basis, or the color of the other cars involved in the collision.

I find it amusing that people find these reactions to a car wreck perfectly acceptable but often assign ill motives to a LEO's similar account of a shooting. Absent a perceived threat, the body does not have time to respond by gearing up for the fight. Oftentimes, the reactions listed above are typical even though the driver's stress response was *post*-impact. Put another way, they are reacting to the event itself and *not* the stress that preceded the event. This is the critical difference between a car wreck and an OIS or other critical incident in which the *pre-event* stress can be overwhelming.

> So he had that little .25 in his hand, and I remember the flash, smell of the gunpowder. It felt like somebody just slugged me in my chin. I couldn't believe I'd been shot! I thought, 'did he shoot me or hit me?' I put my hand up, checked my chin, saw the blood on my hand, I was thought, 'He shot me! That SOB shot me!'
>
> –Name withheld

Many, if not most, OISs involve protracted stressful events such as vehicle pursuits, foot pursuits, armed stand offs, hostage situations, or active physical struggles.

Nearly all involve a stressful response to the scene of the event. This stress *precedes* the use of force. Therefore, it is reasonable to expect that the LEO involved in a critical incident would have a more intense response to the event than the person who was involved in a car crash. The question is, "Why?"

I believe the reason is simple. The human body has the ability to perceive and react to many things simultaneously. However, when the signals received by the body from all five senses lead our minds to conclude that a dangerous situation exists such that our very survival is threatened, our minds focus only on the situation at hand. This necessarily results in the exclusion of other events taking place. Some focus on the threat exclusively while some focus on the solution to the threat. However, our brains place "all hands on deck" to address the immediate matter at hand. This is true not only of LEOs. Read below the account of a true American hero.

The President of the United States in the name of The Congress takes pleasure in presenting the Medal of Honor to: WILLIAMS, HERSHEL WOODROW Corporal, U.S. Marine Corps Reserve, 21st Marines, 3d Marine Division. *Place and date*: Iwo Jima, Volcano Islands, 23 February 1945.

Citation: For conspicuous gallantry and intrepidity at the risk of his life above and beyond the call of duty as demolition sergeant serving with the 21st Marines, 3d Marine Division, in action against enemy Japanese forces on Iwo Jima, Volcano Islands, 23 February 1945. Quick to volunteer his services when our tanks were maneuvering vainly to open a lane for the infantry through the network of reinforced concrete pillboxes, buried mines, and black volcanic sands, Cpl. Williams daringly went forward alone to attempt the reduction of devastating machinegun fire from the unyielding positions. Covered only by 4 riflemen, he fought desperately for 4 hours under terrific enemy small-arms fire and repeatedly returned to his own lines to prepare demolition charges and obtain serviced flamethrowers, struggling back, frequently to the rear of hostile emplacements, to wipe out 1 position after another. On 1 occasion, he daringly mounted a pillbox to insert the nozzle of his flamethrower through the air vent, killing the occupants and silencing the gun; on another he grimly charged enemy riflemen who attempted to stop him with bayonets and destroyed them with a burst of flame from his weapon. His unyielding determination and extraordinary heroism in the face of ruthless enemy resistance were directly instrumental in neutralizing one of the most fanatically defended Japanese strong points encountered by his regiment and aided vitally in enabling his company to reach its objective. Cpl. Williams' aggressive fighting spirit and valiant devotion to duty throughout this fiercely contested action sustain and enhance the highest traditions of the U.S. Naval Service.

During an interview, Herschel "Woody" Williams stated that he does not recall returning to his own front line to retrieve demolition devices and flame throwers during his assault of multiple Japanese pillboxes on Iwo Jima on February 23, 1945. His actions took place during *a period of more than four hours.* He was twenty-two years old at the time. It is clear that the stress of the event caused his body and mind to focus so intently on the threat and the mission to save lives, while staying alive, that his memories are not vivid as one might expect.

Mr. Williams' experience and those of our brave armed forces are fundamentally different from those of LEOs in one critical respect. It is very rare for the actual shooting during an armed confrontation in a law enforcement context to continue for any appreciable length of time. The time from the start of the contact between the suspect and the LEO through the end of the deadly confrontation is many times less than one minute. However, the stress during that time period is intense and potentially overwhelming.

I defended a LEO who was assaulted on a traffic stop by a convicted felon who attempted to take his gun away from him. The officer was engaged in a fight for his life. The confrontation ended when the officer broke free of the suspect, drew his weapon, and the suspect lunged at the officer in another attempt to disarm him. The officer fired one shot and the suspect immediately fell to the ground. The entire confrontation, from the time the LEO exited his vehicle to the time the shot was fired totaled twenty-seven *seconds*. During one half of one minute, this LEO went from the standard alert state of a traffic stop, through an exhausting fight for his life, through the shooting of a suspect.

Through proper physical and mental preparation as well as knowledge and training, you will have sufficient time to react in most situations[7]. However, you do not

---

[7] The ambush of LEOs, such as the execution of four Lakewood, WA police officers in 2009, has become more prevalent and presents a different scenario. In those situations, the LEOs did not have time to react to the threat. LEOs must learn from these incidents and have at least one LEO designated to respond to a threat when several LEOs are gathered for meals, ceremonies, or training. In my opinion, disarming LEOs during such events is reckless and will eventually expose an agency to liability.

have time to hesitate. You must be trained and prepared to act. You must be mentally prepared for the confrontation and have the will to survive.

> *Q: The officer must have the mindset that if they get a chance to defend themselves or a third party they've got to act without hesitation.*
>
> *A: Right and I mean there's been uncountable stories and studies from the professional psychologists who have done their studies and shown people who had a will to survive and they received fatal injuries but had a will to survive and at least survived long enough to take down their assailant. There are other people who have received what would technically be non-fatal injuries but in their minds they were shot, they're supposed to die and they have died from what would typically not be a fatal injury. And then there's the people who live on and either (a) as police officers take down their assailant or (b) as suspects continue to shoot or kill police officers after receiving fatal wounds. They just don't die for maybe thirty seconds to a couple of minutes and take down more police officers.*
>
> –Thirty-two year veteran of law enforcement

Survival is more than a rigid calculus of the number of blows landed, the number of shots fired, or the medical descriptions of the injuries sustained. LEOs need to be concerned with survival first. Hesitation due to the fear of a lawsuit can have deadly consequences.

CHAPTER THREE
LAWFUL USE OF FORCE
AS A LEGAL DEFENSE

He's crouched down in the window, the detective with me is looking in the binoculars and the detective says, "Tom, he's got the hammer cocked back, he's pointing at them." And I realized he's looking at the two officers and they're standing up in view of him. Figuring the way he's taking careful aim at them...I yelled at them "Get down!" or something to that effect...At that point, I had my AR15 rifle. Back then we didn't have patrol rifles but I had one because of being on SWAT, and at that point he just turns the gun towards me and, of course like I said, he already had the hammer cocked back, he's taking careful aim and when I yell at them to get down they drop, he rotates the gun barrel towards me and so that's when I shot him and his head was slightly behind some curtains. I estimated where I thought that area of his head was that I needed to hit. Since he had the hammer cocked, I didn't want the muscle reflexes going off, pulling the trigger on the gun. And so I shot through the curtain into his head. SWAT arrived; we never heard anything else out of him. [Note: The Suspect was found dead with the cocked revolver in his hand]

–Name withheld

Let me paint a picture for you. You are on patrol and are dispatched to a fight in progress in the food court of your local mall. You arrive and run into the mall. You see that the food court is virtually empty except for a few people cowering under the tables. You see one man laying motionless on the ground. He has bright red stains on his shirt. Another man is standing over him holding a gun in a classic two-handed grip. The clothing of both men is disheveled and it appears they have been fighting. In addition, some of the furniture has been turned over. You draw your weapon and approach the two men as you advise radio of the situation and request an EMS response.

What crimes are you considering? Murder? Aggravated assault? Armed robbery? Aggravated battery? Attempted kidnapping?

Now let's change the scenario. The person holding the gun is wearing a law enforcement uniform. What crimes are you considering now?

The use of force in the law enforcement context takes three forms. First is the use of force to effect an arrest. Second is the use of force to protect the LEO. Third is the use of force to protect a third person. Now, many will argue that any use of force by a LEO is intended to effect an arrest. Their argument follows this pattern: When a person uses force against a LEO or a third person and a LEO responds, that LEO is effecting an arrest. This is true because any action to stop the attack or control the perpetrator is done to effect an arrest. However, consider that the same is true when a private citizen uses force. The difference is that a private citizen has the choice to abandon any effort to effect an arrest. A LEO is *always* focused on the ultimate goal of fulfilling her oath of office and completing the arrest of the suspect[8].

Use of Force, Defenses to Prosecution and Justification

When a LEO is accused of improperly using force against a person, the allegation begins with an analysis of the purpose of the force. Was the force used to maintain order, effect an arrest, defend the LEO from an attack, or defend a third party. This is a critical part of the analysis. Another critical part of this analysis is the statutory authority for the use of force.

Nearly every state has a statute that justifies the use of force by LEOs. The Model Penal Code also discusses the use of deadly force by LEOs. See MPC §3.04 Use of Force in Self-Protection & §3.07 Use of Force In Law Enforcement. For ease of discussion, we will use the Georgia statute. I encourage you to review the specific statutes in your home state or jurisdiction.

O.C.G.A. (Official Code of Georgia Annotated) § 17-4-20 reads, in relevant part:

> (b)Sheriffs and peace officers who are appointed or employed in conformity with [Georgia law] *may use deadly force* to apprehend a suspected felon *only when the officer reasonably believes that the suspect possesses a deadly weapon or any object, device, or instrument which, when used offensively against a person, is likely to or actually does result in serious bodily injury;*

---

[8] This is why a suspect should ALWAYS be handcuffed and then searched following an OIS. The failure to do so could allow the suspect to retrieve a concealed weapon and engage the LEOs again.

when the *officer reasonably believes that the suspect poses an immediate threat of physical violence to the officer or others;* or when there is *probable cause to believe that the suspect has committed a crime involving the infliction or threatened infliction of serious physical harm.* Nothing in this Code section shall be construed so as to restrict such sheriffs or peace officers from the *use of such reasonable nondeadly force as may be necessary to apprehend and arrest a suspected felon or misdemeanant.*

(c) Nothing in this Code section shall be construed so as to restrict the use of deadly force by employees of state and county correctional institutions, jails, and other places of lawful confinement or by peace officers of any agency in the State of Georgia when reasonably necessary to prevent escapes or apprehend escapees from such institutions.

(d) No law enforcement agency of this state or of any political subdivision of this state shall adopt or promulgate any rule, regulation, or policy which prohibits a peace officer from using that degree of force to apprehend a suspected felon which is allowed by the statutory and case law of this state. (Emphasis added).

Further authority for the use of force is found in the Georgia code that applies to civilians as well. You will also find a similar statute in your state and should review it. O.C.G.A. §16-3-21 reads, in relevant part, as follows:

(a) A person is justified in threatening or using force against another when and to the extent that he or she *reasonably believes* that such threat or force is necessary to defend himself or herself or a third person against such other's *imminent use of unlawful force*; however, except as provided in Code Section 16-3-23[9], a *person is justified in using force which is intended or likely to cause death or great bodily harm only if he or she reasonably believes that such force is necessary to prevent death or great bodily injury to himself or herself or a third person or to prevent the commission of a forcible felony.* (Emphasis added).

Note that the law regarding the use of deadly force in self-defense or the defense of others is the same for LEOs and civilians. The standard for civilians will likely apply to LEOs who use deadly force while off-duty or out of their home state.

The important thing to consider is that these code sections provide legal *justification* for your actions. A justification[10] is defined as a "[j]ust lawful excuse or reason for an act or failing to act." The burden is on the LEO to show that her actions were justified[11]. Georgia law codifies

---

[9] O.C.G.A. §16-3-23 relates to the use of deadly force in defense of a habitation.
[10] Black's Law Dictionary 9th Ed. (2009) (Justification)
[11] "In any prosecution based on conduct that is justifiable under this Article, justification is an affirmative." MPC §3.01. See also O.C.G.A. §16-3-20 & O.C.G.A. §16-3-28.

this principle at O.C.G.A. §16-3-20 which is printed, in relevant part, below:

> The fact that a person's conduct is justified is a defense to prosecution for any crime based on that conduct. The defense of justification can be claimed:
>
> (1) When the person's conduct is justified under Code Section 16-3-21, 16-3-23, 16-3-24, 16-3-25, or 16-3-26;
>
> (2) *When the person's conduct is in reasonable fulfillment of his duties as a government officer or employee;* . . .
>
> (4) *When the person's conduct is reasonable and is performed in the course of making a lawful arrest*[.] (Emphasis added).

A LEO always bears the burden of proving that her actions were justified in any use of force analysis. The import of this fact is that absent such justification, the LEO can be prosecuted for the use of force. As will be discussed in Chapter Four, entitled, "The Criminal Investigation," it is critical that important facts, including witness statements, be made available to justify your use of force. The investigators must also gather evidence from the scene and ensure that it is properly preserved to accurately portray what occurred.

It is now easy to see how the use of force by a LEO can turn into a prosecution. Consider, for example, an OIS without a death. In Georgia, intentionally shooting another person constitutes an Aggravated Assault. The relevant statute, O.C.G.A. § 16-5-21, reads in relevant part:

(a) A person commits the offense of aggravated assault when he or she assaults:

...

(2) With a deadly weapon or with any object, device, or instrument which, when used offensively against a person, is likely to or actually does result in serious bodily injury[.]

So, in the case of an OIS, we have an intentional shooting of another person and an assault upon another with a deadly weapon. Absent a justification for those actions, the prosecutor may consider bringing charges against the LEO for Aggravated Assault. It is only after having the information surrounding the shooting that the prosecutor is able to make the decision that the OIS was *justified*. It is interesting to note that the same analysis applies in the case of a shooting by a civilian.

Do you now understand why it is important to have an attorney involved before you make any statements to investigators? You will see this point even more clearly as you read the chapters on the criminal and administrative investigations.

Analysis of the Use of Force

I divide the use of force into three categories for the purpose of this discussion, because few people, if any, will dispute that a LEO can use force to effect an arrest. However, the use of force by LEOs to protect themselves or a third party leads to the majority of controversy involving LEOs.

For example, when a LEO places a person under arrest for DUI after a field sobriety evaluation and the suspect begins to fight, few will question the LEO's use of force to *complete* the arrest process. However, this is often not the case when a LEO is attacked immediately after arriving on the scene of a call or traffic stop and is not actively in the process of arresting a suspect when the attack begins. I believe this is also the case when the LEO uses force, especially deadly force, to protect a third person.

The reason for this disconnect is two-fold. The first is poor articulation of the facts in the reports of the LEO and the agency. The second is that agencies do not take advantage of opportunities to control the dialogue following a critical incident in order to educate the public and the media and correct the distorted public perception of the law surrounding the use of force.

Say It, Then Document It

The first concern can be remedied easily. The report should indicate that the suspect was told at least once that he was under arrest—during the fight with a LEO, while he was holding a weapon, or when he was threatening a person during a domestic dispute. LEOs should tell the suspect he is under arrest along with commands to stop resisting. Then the LEO's report should articulate the following: the LEO told the suspect he was under arrest, the probable cause for the particular crime or crimes, and the specific laws the LEO was attempting to enforce. Consider the following scenario as an example of the principle articulated above.

A LEO approaches a group of people on a report of a domestic disturbance. One of the people shoves the LEO and tells him to leave because he does not have a warrant. The LEO is authorized, and should, use force to protect herself and take the suspect into custody. We cannot predict the amount of force necessary to effect the arrest as the *degree of resistance is always solely within the control of the suspect.* However, it is reasonable to conclude that such a suspect will not give up quickly. It is also easy to articulate that the LEO is also acting to protect herself from physical harm and to prevent the suspect from disarming her. Every encounter with a LEO is an armed encounter. So, the LEO should attempt to gain control of the suspect as quickly as possible.

The LEO in our scenario immediately tells the suspect he is under arrest. She next tells him to get on the ground, put his hands behind his back, etc. If he resists her efforts, she should tell him to stop resisting and continue to give him commands to clearly indicate what he should do to comply. She should, when possible, continue to tell him he is under arrest.

Irrespective of the amount of force used to effect the arrest, or the number of LEOs needed, the suspect will be placed under control and arrested at some point. So, in her report she should detail the fact that she clearly articulated to the suspect that he was under arrest early during the confrontation. She should also detail the probable cause that existed at the time she placed the suspect under arrest and the crimes for which she placed him under arrest. As she continues to detail the events, she should relate the suspect's response, verbal and physical, not only to the efforts to effect his arrest, but also upon being advised that he was under arrest.

Over the past twenty years, defensive tactics have come a long way. By incorporating real world statistics and video footage of attacks on LEOs, instructors have changed the way LEOs respond to threats. Encouraging LEOs to close the gap to control a physical confrontation, recognizing that every confrontation is an armed confrontation due to the number of LEOs who are disarmed, and immediately using an appropriate level of force are all techniques that have kept LEOs safe and prevented many situations from escalating.

As part of this trend, instructors have taught LEOs to give verbal commands during physical confrontations. The goal is to make it clear to the suspect exactly what you want them to do. This also has the effect of helping to coordinate the efforts of several LEOs as they work together to secure a suspect. From high risk traffic stops to passively-resisting suspects during misdemeanor arrests, communicating with the suspect has become a common occurrence in law enforcement. "Stop resisting," "Give me your hands," and "Turn on your stomach" all communicate to the suspect exactly what is expected during a confrontation.

As we all know, there is another benefit to giving loud verbal commands and instructions. If the encounter is observed by witnesses or recorded on video, observers will be able to relate that the LEOs were being professional and continuing to make it clear to the suspect exactly what was expected of him. I would like to suggest that LEOs add another phrase to their training: "You're under arrest[12]!"

In any situation, initial or continued resistance constitutes a criminal act. By communicating to the suspect that he is under arrest, he can no longer justify resisting on

---

[12] Giving commands also forces you to breathe during the physical confrontation to avoid running out of oxygen in your bloodstream.

the grounds that he was not aware that the LEOs were in fact officers or that he was being placed under arrest. Second, resistance after being advised he is under arrest will justifiably lead to further charges.

In my experience, the public, namely jurors, will support a LEO who is effecting an arrest. However, in many of the videos I see, LEOs do not tell the suspect he is under arrest until after he is under control, in handcuffs and in the back of a patrol vehicle. This is especially true when the LEO is attacked. This can lead to allegations that the suspect was confused about what was happening. So, make it clear and tell the suspect, "You're under arrest!" Upon hearing those words, any law-abiding citizen would and should stop resisting.

The last step is to document the events in your incident report. Document that you told the suspect he was under arrest, as well as the probable cause for the charges, such as simple battery, obstruction of a LEO, assault, etc. Make it clear to anyone reviewing your actions that the suspect was not only told to comply with your commands and was told exactly what you wanted him to do, but that he was also told early in the confrontation that he was under arrest. This will also make for powerful testimony at trial.

The fact that a person is under arrest is apparently not as obvious as you would expect. I remember when our county jail installed a huge sign in the intake area. It simply said, "You are in jail." While this should not have been a revelation to any suspect after being told he was under arrest and taking a ride in the back of a patrol car *in handcuffs*, some folks were genuinely surprised to learn this was the destination all along. Go figure. Perhaps they thought they were heading to the ballgame.

CHAPTER FOUR
THE CRIMINAL INVESTIGATION

Q: Did you call an attorney to the scene? Did you ask for an attorney to represent you?

A: No, and it was never even a thought. It was never even something that crossed my mind.

–Name withheld

If you are a LEO, your conversations with other LEOs do not typically begin with these words, "You have the right to remain silent." However, every OIS will result in a criminal investigation conducted by other LEOs. While many agencies ask an outside agency to conduct the criminal investigation into an OIS, in many cases, those LEOs are friends, former beat partners, or people who were in your academy class when you started the profession. Aside from the stress of the shooting itself, sitting in a room with one or two criminal investigators can be one of the worst experiences for a LEO.

The most important thing for any LEO to remember during the criminal investigation is the first few words of the Miranda warning: You have the *right* to remain silent. You are not required to speak with any criminal investigator about the shooting. If you choose not to speak with the criminal investigators, you cannot be disciplined or fired and your silence cannot be used against you in any criminal proceeding[13]. This is your right under the United States Constitution and likely under your state constitution[14] as well.

There are three critical decisions for every LEO regarding a statement to criminal investigators following an OIS. I believe the first and most critical decision is the timing of the statement. As you can see from the statements of LEOs placed throughout this book, you may not be in any condition to provide a coherent statement to criminal investigators within twenty-four hours of an OIS. You should NEVER give a statement to anyone, especially criminal investigators, if you are overwhelmed, tired, or

---

[13] *Miranda v. Arizona* 384 U.S. 436 (1966)
[14] *Self-incrimination:* No person shall be compelled to give testimony tending in any manner to be self-incriminating. Ga. Const. Art. I, §I. Para. VVI.

not in control of your emotions. The second decision is whether you will insist on having counsel present. After all, as the Miranda warning states, "You have the right to have an attorney present during any questioning." This is also a right guaranteed by the United States Constitution. Finally, should you simply make a statement, answer questions, or put a time limit on the interview? These decisions begin with an understanding of a concept that bears repeating: statements to criminal investigators and participation in a criminal investigation following an OISs are *voluntary*.

Many LEOs believe they do not need an attorney if the OIS is "a good shoot." As I tell LEOs, you will always believe it is "a good shoot" because *you made the decision to use deadly force.* Your perceptions, beliefs, physical condition, and many other factors enter into your decision to shoot. However, people will second guess your decision without the stress of the event while enjoying the luxury of time. In short, I always recommend that LEOs have an attorney come to the scene of an OIS and meet with them prior to any statements to any entity.

Timing of the Interview or Statement

The time period immediately following an OIS can be hectic. *If* the LEO encounters a single suspect, the use of force ends the confrontation, *and* the LEO is not injured, it is relatively easy to define a beginning and end point to the encounter. Investigators can then secure the scene, gather important personnel, secure the LEO, and provide a safe, stress-free environment for the LEO. In this scenario, the LEO has time to contact a family member to ensure they know the LEO is OK, contact a spiritual advisor if desired, and take the time to decompress and meet with counsel. In a country with well-trained LEOs, this is fortunately the typical OIS scenario. However, this is not always the case.

OISs occur in all types of environments, including interstates, mass transit trains and stations, schools, shopping malls, wooded areas, and any other environment to which LEOs are called to protect and serve. In addition, many OISs involve more than one perpetrator and more than one LEO. Further, although any use of force ideally ends with the suspect in custody and the LEO safe, this is not always the case. One or more LEOs may be injured or killed. The suspect may flee, may be injured, unharmed, or be taken from the scene by emergency medical personnel in an unknown condition. It is important to remember that if the LEO fires a shot and the suspect leaves the scene unharmed, this is still considered an OIS involving the use of deadly force.

When the scene is not easily secured, when the location or condition of the suspect is not known, or when a LEO is injured or killed, the timing of the statement to criminal investigators becomes complicated. As a LEO, you must provide information that can help identify a suspect who has left the scene to aid in his capture and help secure medical treatment if he is injured. Further, your statements to investigators will help them secure evidence necessary to provide a clear picture of what occurred.

In every OIS, there is some information that investigators need to start the investigative process. Questions such as "What did the suspect do when you arrived?," "What did you do, say, or hear upon arrival?," and "Where were you and the suspect located when the shooting occurred?" seek basic facts. Providing this information[15] not only assists the investigators in understanding your perceptions at the time of the shooting, it also provides critical information needed to secure the scene and gather evidence.

While some attorneys who represent LEOs advise their clients not to make any statements at all to any investigators at any time, I disagree. Following the shooting, the investigators will be gathering evidence. They will photograph you and they will take custody of your weapon[16] and any other equipment used during the encounter. You must be prepared for these activities. You must also be prepared for the fact that you will be separated from your patrol vehicle. You will need to ask the investigators to secure your personal effects such as your keys, wallet, and phone for you to take with you when you go home. In short, you will be having some dialogue with the criminal investigators at some point. Without some advance consideration of what you will say, you may talk uncontrollably under the stress of the event.

The stress of the critical incident will affect you physically and emotionally. Expect it, prepare for it.

After the second or third round, I actually looked at the shotgun and I thought, 'Am I shooting blanks?'

–Name withheld

---

[15] Some call this a "scene walk thru" and many times, this is done with the attorney for the LEO. In some instances, the LEO relates information to the attorney who in turn speaks to the investigators.

[16] It is important to always issue another weapon to the LEO immediately. First, the removal of a weapon from a LEO can give the impression she has acted improperly. Second, the LEO is still on duty and must be able to protect herself or others. This is especially true if the LEO remains at the scene or is in uniform.

Following an OIS, LEOs describe periods of distraction, uncontrollable emotions and extreme fatigue. In my experience, LEOs often recall very little of the interviews given within twenty-four hours after an OIS. In short, the uncontrollable physiological responses to the extreme stress of an OIS will, more than likely, impair your ability to listen to questions, understand those questions, remain focused on the interview and provide coherent and complete answers. Even if you are able to provide a coherent statement, you should get adequate rest prior to a comprehensive interview.

> *If I ever shoot anybody again or anybody under my command ever shoots anybody, they will go home. They will not be kept here for eight hours and put through that interview, this interview and write this report.*
>
> *There's no rush. You can get your initial report, just initial 'this is what happened' and let him go home, take him home, stay with him, get them with their family. If they don't have a family, put somebody with them and don't bring them in and start doing these interviews.*
>
> —Name withheld

It is important to understand the role of the criminal investigators. First and foremost, they are charged with gathering all evidence. Use of force in the real world does not take place in a confined area. Struggles with suspects can cover large areas including many rooms of a house, several properties such as in a foot chase, or many miles of highway during a vehicle pursuit. Investigators will need some information from you to secure the scene or multiple scenes relevant to the investigation. Remember that evidence comes in all forms. Some evidence is temporary, such as footprints, and some can be removed from the scene by bystanders. The bottom line is that you will not be able to gather evidence necessary to present a clear picture of what occurred and clear yourself, nor will anyone on your behalf without some information. Therefore, you must transmit some information to the criminal investigators to protect yourself. You can do this through counsel if your attorney is present at the scene. This is all part of the most important role of the criminal investigators: determining whether the use of force complied with state law.

Once the scene has been secured and the investigators can begin processing the evidence, you can decide whether to provide any further information. I always recommend that the LEO take time to decompress and process what has occurred before giving any further statements to criminal investigators. The research regarding LEOs involved in critical incidents is clear. It can take up to seventy-two hours to process the sounds of gunshots and to recall what occurred during an OIS[17]. Therefore, you should wait to give detailed accounts of what occurred. I have represented LEOs who were incapable of giving a statement within hours of an event. They were too emotional, and either filled with too much adrenaline or too fatigued to answer questions in a coherent manner. As a general rule, federal agents do not speak with anyone for at least seventy-two hours following a shooting.

---

[17] See generally Administrative Investigations of Police Shootings and Other Critical Incidents: Officer Statements and Use of Force Reports Part One: Prologue 2008 (6) AELE Mo. L. J. 201

The final consideration regarding the timing of the statement relates to the condition of the suspect. Never give a statement beyond the basics outlined above regarding the location of evidence without knowing the condition of the suspect. First, there is a difference between providing a statement in an OIS when the suspect sustains minor injuries as opposed to a situation involving a suspect who died from his injuries. Second, you must have an opportunity to process the condition of the suspect prior to giving a statement. I've sat with LEOs after a shooting and insisted that the criminal investigators tell me the suspect's condition. Although I suspected that the suspect expired, neither my client nor I was certain. Immediately following the shooting, as is often the case, the suspect was aided by backup officers and immediately taken from the scene in an ambulance. If you enter an interview room to give a statement and learn for the first time that the suspect died, your spontaneous reaction and statements could paint a picture of you as a remorseful person who regrets his actions and is unable to control his emotions. Those reactions and statements will be captured on audio and video and will forever be a part of the case file. You will see that video again in any civil case that arises from the use of force.

Give yourself a chance to make a coherent statement that accurately reflects the events and your perceptions. Be informed about the suspect's condition and the condition of other LEOs who were on the scene and be certain that you are physically and emotionally able to make a statement. Remember this rule: The statement you make is the one you will deal with for many years to come in criminal and civil inquiries about the shooting.

Finally, it is important to ensure all rounds fired are accounted for before you provide a statement to criminal investigators. Bullets will stop somewhere. What if the round you fired missed the suspect and struck a person next door? Could you be charged with manslaughter or reckless conduct? I routinely wait until the investigators confirm that no other victims were found and all projectiles were accounted for before I will allow my client to provide a statement to criminal investigators.

The Right to Counsel

I periodically receive requests for information regarding on-scene response for attorneys. This is one of my favorite topics, and I gave a presentation on this issue to the Annual General Counsel's Conference for the Fraternal Order of Police a few years ago.

I strongly encourage LEOs to have an attorney respond to the scene if they are involved in critical incidents. This advice extends to more than officer involved shootings. For instance, an on-duty car wreck that results in serious injuries should prompt an on-scene attorney response. This also applies to *any* in-custody death of a suspect.

Having an attorney respond to the scene does not happen without some advanced planning. My home FOP lodge, Georgia State Lodge 13, is developing a "critical incident card" with emergency phone numbers. Many LEOs simply provide the numbers for counsel to their 911 center and rely on the emergency operators to contact an attorney to respond to the scene. I have also been flattered to hear that I am "on speed dial" for many LEOs. However you decide to structure the system, make certain you are able to contact the attorney of your choice on a twenty-four hour basis.

Calling your favorite member of the bar at three in the morning is only half of the equation. Will he be able to get to the scene? Does she have credentials to get through the outer perimeter? Does he have a good working relationship with your command staff? Most important, does your command staff view your attorney on the scene as a good thing or a sign of the apocalypse?

> *Q: Did you ever think about calling a lawyer when you were getting into your interviews?*
>
> *A: I didn't; never did. If I had to do it today, you'd be with me.*

Here are several important points of any plan that will help provide the LEOs in your agency with an on-scene response from an attorney.

1. Make certain you can contact your attorney twenty-four hours per day. You work morning watch. Your attorney should, too.

2. Provide a system that will allow others to contact your counsel for you. You may be injured, your cell phone may be disabled after a fight or remain unavailable in your patrol vehicle, or you may be on an inner perimeter for an extended period of time after a shooting.

3. Provide your counsel some type of credentials. This can be a business card or an identification card with a photo.

4. Discuss the on-scene response of an attorney with your chain of command. Let them know that your intent is to protect the agency and the individual LEO.

5. Incorporate the on-scene response of counsel into your critical incident plans.

I have represented several LEOs who shot unarmed suspects. They all involved the lawful use of deadly force. In each of those cases, I heard from members of the command staff who were happy to have me there. My presence was the result of planning and coordination. This can be a challenge if you use deadly force outside of your jurisdiction while carrying a firearm pursuant to the Law Enforcement Officers Safety Act (LEOSA)[18]. Plan ahead and carry the numbers of the local FOP lodge where you are traveling or call your home lodge counsel who can assist in finding an attorney for you in any jurisdiction near your travel location.

You are no different from any other person interviewed by criminal investigators[19]. You have a right to have counsel present to observe the process, advise you regarding the questions asked, your responses, and whether to continue the interview. I have found that most LEOs, even seasoned veterans, are not prepared for the events that will occur during an interview with criminal investigators following an OIS. Therefore, I will take some time to outline what you can expect. As you read ahead, you may learn some facts, but more likely you will be

---

[18] 18 USC 926B & 926C.

[19] "We conclude that policemen, like teachers and lawyers, are not relegated to a watered-down version of constitutional rights." *Garrity v. State of N.J.*, 385 U.S. 493, 479, 87 S. Ct. 616, 620, 17 L. Ed. 2d 562 (1967)

reminded of the fact that this interview, like any other criminal investigation, is not the same as sitting with a friend casually speaking about your day in a squad room.

This is an investigation with trained and often seasoned investigators. They will read Miranda-type warnings to you and likely have you sign an acknowledgment and waiver of those warnings. The investigators will likely be senior ranking members of your agency or may be from another agency. The practice of bringing in an outside agency to investigate OISs is becoming more common. In addition, the shooting may occur outside your jurisdiction after a pursuit, while you are off-duty in another state, or while you are carrying a firearm pursuant to the LEOSA. Therefore, you should consider that you may or may not know the investigators.

Here is a typical scenario. The interview will take place in an interview room in a law enforcement agency building. Now, we all know how quickly news travels in a law enforcement agency. Therefore, you can count on being the subject of stares and glances on the way to and from the interview room. The room will probably be small and cramped due to the number of investigators in the room. The interview will be audio and video recorded, although the microphone and camera may be concealed. There also may be a concealed viewing window, through which command staff and senior investigators will likely watch and listen to the interview.

During the interview, you will probably be asked to draw a diagram of the relevant scene or areas. The investigators will ask where you were standing, your relative position to the suspect, and how many times you fired. This is a critical point as you truly may not recall how many times you fired. Further, when asked what you said to the suspect, whether you or other LEOs on the scene gave verbal commands, or what, if anything, the suspect said to you, you may find yourself unable to answer. The problem is that, well before you use deadly force, you will experience auditory exclusion[20]. Therefore, it might take several days for you to recall what was said, and you may never truly be able to accurately recall that information.

Q: What type of rifle and bullet were you using?
A: A .308 Federal 180 grain boat tail hollow point, I think.

Q: Was the rifle suppressed?
A: No.

Q: Did you hear it go off?
A: I did not. It was like a bubble that came over me. All I could hear was him yelling and it was muted. I could hear my heart beat. When I unbolted and bolted for a second shot, I heard every click of that bolt and that empty brass round coming out and actually hitting the dirt. Those were vivid sounds to me, but I never heard the shot. My ears didn't even ring afterwards.

–Name withheld

---

[20] Auditory exclusion is a psychological reaction to intense stress that limits the perceived hearing of the LEO. This is similar to the perceived distortions of time and perception of events that accompany high stress.

In states that are fortunate enough to have a Peace Officer's Bill of Rights, you may have the right to secure someone to represent you in any meeting with investigators. However, in every criminal investigation, you have a right to counsel under the United States Constitution.

Statements to Others

Be very careful with statements made to individuals who are not investigators. Those statements may be used by the prosecution unless they are protected by a legal privilege. For instance, statements made to your spouse are generally privileged[21]. Statements made to an attorney are privileged unless the attorney is an employee of the law enforcement agency or a prosecutor[22]. In some states, statements made to pastors, priests, and religious counselors are privileged if you are seeking spiritual guidance, but this is not the case in all states[23]. As to peer counselors, only a few states provide immunity for such statements[24]. Finally, statements to psychiatrists and psychologists are generally privileged, unless the statements are made to a professional employed by the law enforcement agency or the government[25]. In short, be careful to whom you speak after a critical incident. In general, privileges are strictly construed, which means that it is very easy to make a mistake and breach the

---

[21] This is known generally as the marital privilege. O.C.G.A. § 24-9-21(1) & O.C.G.A. § 24-9-23

[22] Federal Rule of Evidence 502.

[23] O.C.G.A. § 24-9-22; O.C.G.A. § 24-5-502 (effective 01/01/13)

[24] Examples: CO (C.R.S.A. § 13-90-107); HI (HRS § 78-52); LA (LSA-C.E. Art. 518); MN (M.S.A. § 181.973); NC (N.C.G.S.A. § 8-53.10); ND (NDCC §32-03-48); OK (12 Okl.St.Ann. § 2506.2); OR (O.R.S. § 181.860); WA (RCWA 5.60.060);

[25] O.C.G.A. § 24-9-21(5-8)

privilege. Consult your attorney prior to speaking with anyone about a critical incident.

Where you speak to someone is just as important. The law generally presumes that there is no right to privacy or privilege with regard to statements made in public and within the hearing of others[26]. For example, the statements to your lawyer in a crowded elevator at the courthouse may not be privileged.

Perhaps of most concern are statements made to other LEOs. Except in extremely limited circumstances, such as LEOs who are married to LEOs or statements made to a pastor who is employed by the agency, such statements are not privileged. I have seen this become an issue when the LEO either speaks with a friend or seeks assistance with the legal process by appealing to the Executive Board of her local Fraternal Order of Police Lodge. If you must make a statement to secure funds for legal representation, be extremely general or have your attorney address the board on your behalf. If you are not careful, the members of the Executive Board can be forced to reveal exactly what you related about the incident.

Let's be clear about something. I am not concerned about your statements to these individuals. I am concerned about the ability of these individuals to *accurately recall* exactly what you said. This is especially true when any variation in their recollection could mean the difference between being cleared and being indicted.

---

[26] *S. Guar. Ins. Co. of Georgia v. Ash*, 192 Ga. App. 24, 28, 383 S.E.2d 579, 583 (1989).

From Interview to Interrogation

LEOs interview witnesses and people with knowledge. LEOs interrogate suspects[27]. We all know there are other differences between interviews and interrogations. The former is a fact gathering process that should be relaxed, friendly, and non-confrontational. The latter is the polar opposite in terms of environment. Although some interrogations begin in a friendly manner, the goal of an interrogation is to keep the suspect off balance, break down his ability to tell lies, and learn the truth. The environment of an interview is intended to keep the interviewee comfortable and calm, while everything about an interrogation is intended to keep the suspect from getting or staying comfortable. Interviews are intended to reduce stress. Interrogations focus on increasing psychological stress[28]. Following a critical incident, no LEO should be interrogated—*EVER*! Unless and until evidence is obtained that leads investigators to *objectively* believe that the LEO committed a crime, any and all meetings with investigators should be conducted as interviews.

Now, some critics will have a lot to say about the statements in the preceding paragraph, so I'll address their concerns here. In short, I will destroy the nonsensical arguments of uninformed, ignorant, and silly people who believe LEOs should be treated like any other suspect following a critical incident, especially an OIS. As you can tell, I am very passionate about this topic. My passion comes from speaking with LEOs after shootings, watching them shake and cry when they learn the suspect who tried to kill them died from gunshot wounds, and praying with them while they thanked God that they will go home to

---

[27] Swanson, C.R. et al, *Criminal Investigations, 6th Ed.* 1996 pp. 224 & 225.
[28] Id.

their families. We are all the sum total of our experiences. My biases and beliefs about this subject are my own. I want you to form your own opinions.

Let's look at the reasons, the real and legitimate reasons, for the techniques used during an interrogation. There are essentially five.

1. Gain control of the suspect to prevent escape or flight from the jurisdiction.
2. Increase psychological stress to break down barriers to the truth such as lies and evasive behavior.
3. Quickly obtain admissions and confessions to prevent the destruction of evidence.
4. Secure information regarding co-conspirators and accomplices before they can escape.
5. Establish a set of facts from the suspect that can then be verified, refuted, or tested throughout the remainder of the investigation.

As I will show below, none of the reasons above will justify the interrogation of a LEO following a critical incident, especially an OIS. We will explore each of the reasons cited above. Not only will my explanations show that an interrogation is not necessary, you will see more than enough justification to delay an interview of a LEO following a critical incident, especially an OIS, until the LEO is able to sleep a few nights in a safe environment.

1. Gain control of the suspect to prevent escape or flight from the jurisdiction.

How many times after a shooting does a shooter administer first aid, call the police, advise the exact location of the shooting, request that LEOs respond, remain on the scene, provide his weapon to investigators, pose for photographs without being asked to do so, and return to the law enforcement agency to write a report about what happened? I could go on, but that would be overkill. Enough said.

2. Increase psychological stress to break down barriers to the truth such as lies and evasive behavior.

Following an OIS shooting, I have seen LEOs vomit, cry, shake uncontrollably, shut down, remain unable to speak, and show many other signs of overwhelming stress and accompanying physiological responses. There is no reason to take steps to increase the stress upon a LEO in this situation. Furthermore, any increase in stress will likely push the LEO into a condition where stress prevents even the basic recall of information and communication.

In the next few years, we will have more and more OIS involving officers who are combat veterans. Our wars in Iraq and Afghanistan, as well as any armed conflict in the past fifteen years, have involved a great deal of close quarters combat in urban environments. Although, as a veteran of such combat, you may feel like you have "been there before" following an OIS, you should think again. An OIS will be different. You should expect not only a heightened stress response to such situations, an OIS can have an effect of bringing to mind earlier conflicts and actually raise your stress level above those expected in an OIS. You should have counsel present. As a veteran, you earned that right. Speaking to investigators without the assistance of counsel during this period of heightened stress might impair the investigation, and the agency could be left with a useless and likely misleading statement that will follow the LEO and the agency throughout any related[29] civil litigation.

3. Quickly obtain admissions and confessions to prevent the destruction of evidence.

The agency is in control of all of the evidence following an OIS. The firearm, the uniform, the vehicle, the remaining rounds, the magazines, and more are fully within the control of the agency. You likely have a video of the entire incident.

4. Secure information regarding co-conspirators and accomplices before they can escape.

If you need information regarding the other LEOs on the scene, here are a couple of sources: dispatch records, dash cameras, radio traffic, shift logs, supervisors, work schedules, and the list goes on. None of these potential

---

[29] Remember that any critical incident has the potential to create liability for the agency in relation to any future critical incident. Lawyers typically request files regarding previous incidents that are factually similar to the present suit. Such "similar incidents" are often admissible in a civil trial.

"co-conspirators" and "accomplices" are going anywhere. How many times do you have the name, address, date of birth, social security number, home address, work address, home, work, and cell numbers of potential "co-conspirators" and "accomplices" following a shooting?

5. Establish a set of facts from the suspect that can then be verified, refuted, or tested throughout the remainder of the investigation.

In many instances of homicide or aggravated assault, the statements of the suspect may provide the *only* account of what occurred. This is especially true of the motive for the assault or killing. Aside from the information provided above about the availability of witnesses, dashcam, recordings of radio traffic, and cooperative shooters, I'll help with the motive. The LEO shot or used force to stay alive, save a life or effect an arrest. Pure and simple. No complicated love triangle, insurance schemes, or international conspiracies.

Hopefully, you can now see that there is no reason to interrogate a LEO, especially immediately after an OIS. Sometimes I will allow the LEO to make a statement to homicide investigators, with a few limited follow-up questions. Remember, this is a voluntary interview that you may terminate at any time.

Of course this all changes, and the agency will have a right to push for an interrogation if objective information and evidence leads the agency to believe that an alternative motive exists for the use of force or that the LEO has tampered with evidence. As law enforcement professionals, we should all support the obligations of an agency to investigate criminal activity within their respective jurisdictions. If indeed a LEO has intentionally violated their oath of office and the law, we must police our own.

The Path from Investigation

When the criminal investigation is complete, someone must make a decision as to whether the use of force was lawful. While the administrative investigation will result in a finding of whether the LEO complied with agency policy and law enforcement standards, the criminal investigation is conducted for the purpose of determining if the LEO violated the law. In this respect, the criminal investigation into the use of force is no different from any other criminal investigation.

In my experience, this procedure varies by state and by jurisdiction. The criminal investigators make a determination and state their opinions in their report as to whether the use of force was lawful. In others, the criminal investigators present their findings, facts, and evidence to a prosecutor who will determine how to proceed. Irrespective of the process, at some point, the case will then be in the hands of a prosecutor. This is a good procedure, consistent with our government principle of a separation of powers. Only through such independent reviews will our citizens have faith in our system.

The procedure followed by prosecutors also varies greatly. Some will independently evaluate the case file as received from the criminal investigators and decide whether to prosecute. In other instances, prosecutors present the case to a grand jury. Within the grand jury process, there are also variations. These range from a request for a grand jury recommendation as to whether the prosecutor should continue the investigation, to a formal presentment of charges that includes testimony from the criminal investigators and the LEO[30]. In any case, the suspect and the family of the suspect are generally not permitted to participate in the grand jury proceedings.

You should become familiar with the criminal process in your state. Remember at all times that your participation in the criminal process is voluntary. You are also entitled to counsel at all times. When in doubt about your rights throughout this process, refer to the United States Constitution. As a person under investigation, or being prosecuted, at any stage, you have rights. You should protect yourself by taking advantage of those rights.

Prosecution

It is very rare for a LEO to be prosecuted for improper use of force on a state level. However, it can happen. I will not go into details about defense strategies, how to proceed in the event that a prosecutor decides to prosecute, or a grand jury returns an indictment. Suffice it to say that *any* such action should be taken very seriously. You must secure experienced attorneys to defend you in the criminal case— attorneys experienced in criminal defense and law enforcement procedures. This may require more than one attorney.

Consider that an indictment may force an agency to terminate your employment. This means that your family will be placed under significant financial pressure to secure

---

[30] In Georgia, LEOs have the right to notice and to appear and address a grand jury considering any indictment that relates to an act taken within the course and scope of their employment. See O.C.G.A. § 17-7-52 & O.C.G.A. § 45-11-4.

an attorney to defend you. You must find a way to afford competent representation. You have too much to lose.

It is important to remember that a private citizen may seek to bypass the traditional, established process and seek to prosecute a LEO on their own initiative. For example, most states have a procedure that allows a citizen to seek charges or a warrant for another citizen[31]. I represented a LEO who shot and killed a suspect who tried to kill him. The LEO was cleared by the outside agency that investigated the case and by the district attorney. When the district attorney was criticized for his decision, he decided to present the case to the grand jury. However, before the district attorney could do so, the family of the suspect, assisted by their civil attorney[32], sought a private arrest warrant for the LEO for murder. I represented the LEO in a six-hour hearing. He was cleared of all charges by the judge, who determined that the shooting and killing of the suspect were justified under the law. We won this case because the LEO took the family's attempt to prosecute him seriously from the very outset. As I write this text, he is still on patrol protecting his community, including the people who tried to prosecute him.

Federal Inquiries into the Use of Force

If, as a LEO, you are approached by any investigator other than one working for your agency's internal affairs unit, you should presume that the investigator is engaged in a *criminal* investigation. You should NOT speak with any criminal investigators without first speaking with counsel and having an attorney with you. This is a short

---

[31] See e.g. O.C.G.A. § 17-4-40
[32] The family had previously filed a civil suit in federal court against the LEO and his agency.

section, because the advice is simple: do not speak with criminal investigators without speaking with your attorney first and having him present during any questioning. If the investigators are professional and interested in a pursuit of the truth, they will not mind waiting for you to speak with your attorney first and having your attorney present when they ask you questions. Your agency should NEVER order you to cooperate with a federal investigation. In fact, a LEO cannot be forced to waive Garrity immunity under a criminal investigation[33]. We will discuss Garrity immunity in the next chapter, but simply stated, a statement coerced by the threat of discipline or job loss is not admissible in a criminal court.

---

[33] See *Garner v. Broaderick*, 392 U.S. 273 (1968)

CHAPTER FIVE
THE ADMINISTRATIVE
INVESTIGATION

Q: Do you think one of the roles of the supervisors after a shooting is to look after the officer and protect his rights just like they would anyone else?

A: I think it's probably—I think it's the primary role; taking care of that officer.

–Thirty-two year veteran of law enforcement

You receive a letter that you are under investigation. "I do not need a lawyer yet. I will just see what this is about." You go through the interview and it is pretty intimidating. "I do not need a lawyer yet. I will see if they clear me." You receive a notice to appear before the head of your agency to discuss the results and findings of the investigation. "I do not need a lawyer yet. I'll see what the chief has to say." The chief meets with you, advises the charges were sustained, and she says you have an opportunity to state your case one last time. "I wish I had a lawyer. How did this happen?!"

So you hire a lawyer to appeal the chief's decision. The lawyer will now file the appeal based on the letter you received, the interview you gave, and the meeting you had with the chief. For better or worse, your attorney can only work with the case you hand him.

The role of a lawyer in an internal investigation is complicated. Your rights during investigations may arise from a Peace Officer's Bill of Rights, your state constitution, the United States Constitution, a collective bargaining agreement, or the policies of your agency. Even though the role of an attorney may be limited in many instances, the role of the attorney as a counselor is *never* limited. An attorney can help you ensure that your rights are protected, make certain that you review the appropriate policies and documents prior to making any statements, and help you organize your thoughts.

When you do not involve an attorney until the appeal phase, your attorney is forced to appeal the "record" you hand him. Any missteps you commit along the way will affect the strength of your appeal. In some instances, a mistake on your part could preclude an appeal *entirely*. Administrative deadlines are *hard deadlines*. Missing a deadline affects your rights.

You should begin protecting your appeal rights as soon as you believe you may be subject to discipline. Develop a relationship with an attorney early to make it easier to reach out to him. When it comes to consulting an attorney early, an ounce of prevention is worth a pound of cure.

Confidentiality

More often than not, when a LEO is "under investigation," the entire agency knows about it. Let's face it, as a profession we are good at respecting the privacy rights of the public, but "scoop" on our coworkers is generally fair game. Those casual conversations and the ever churning rumor mill present in many, if not most, agencies create a pitfall for LEOs.

Investigations into misconduct should be conducted in a confidential manner for several reasons. First and foremost, LEOs are professionals. An investigation into misconduct of a fellow professional is a serious matter. Therefore, the details, as well as the existence, of an investigation should be closely guarded to the same degree as a sensitive criminal investigation. Just as a false criminal allegation can destroy the reputation of a private citizen, the mere allegation of misconduct, even if unfounded, can signal the end of a LEO's career.

The second reason to keep these matters confidential is simple; until proven, an allegation is just that and nothing more. Agency administrators are very sensitive to keeping criminal allegations under wraps until investigators possess sufficient probable cause to bring charges against a citizen. The same respect and presumption of innocence must be afforded to LEOs who are under investigation.

Sounds like a due process issue to me, but what do I know. I'm just a lawyer!

The third reason to avoid casual conversations about pending investigations is to protect the integrity of the process. Standard investigative techniques mandate that we separate witnesses to avoid tainting their impressions and potential testimony. When the agency is buzzing with rumors and innuendo about an administrative investigation, you risk tainting the information to be gleaned from interviews. Those tainted statements will surface again in personnel hearings, criminal cases, and lawsuits. By then, it is too late to "un-ring the bell."

Finally, LEOs who are under investigation should beware of casual conversations with anyone. Remember that Garrity protections[34] apply to statements *compelled by management*. Any statements you make to a deputy chief who asks you what happened "off the record" may not be protected under Garrity. If this occurs, you will be required to show a court that you subjectively believed that you were required to answer those questions. I would hope that such "off the record" conversations are not an attempt to entrap you, but I was not born yesterday. This is particularly important in any use of force investigation.

So, here is my advice for administrators and LEOs who are under investigation as well as any LEO in the agency. For the folks in charge, your agency should have a strict policy to keep any allegation of misconduct confidential. This includes investigations conducted by a criminal division, internal affairs, or at the supervisor level. The consequences for failing to keep such allegations confidential should be the same as the consequences for

---

[34] I will discuss the origin and scope of Garrity protections in this chapter.

leaking information on a sensitive criminal investigation to the public.

For the LEOs under investigation, speak only to the investigators and your attorney. Nothing good will come from discussing these matters with your coworkers. At the very least, you may taint the very testimony that can exonerate you. In the worst case scenario, you may place a friend at the center of an investigation that does not concern her. If you are approached by anyone who desires to speak "off the record," you should respectfully decline the opportunity irrespective of the rank of the person who initiates the conversation. Tell them you are under orders from your attorney not to discuss the matter without counsel present. Any lawyer will give you this instruction once the lawyer is engaged to represent you. If you do not have an attorney to assist with your defense of the allegations, perhaps you should reconsider your decision to "go it alone."

For the rest of the LEOs in the agency, preserve and exemplify the highest standards of our profession by respecting the investigative process. Refuse to engage in the idle banter and rumor sharing, and discourage others from doing so. Remember that your "off the record" statement could change the direction of the investigation and become the pivotal piece of evidence in a disciplinary hearing or trial. How will you defend the fact that your statement was based upon a rumor? Most important, recognize that you could be under investigation tomorrow. What level of professionalism would you expect from your fellow professionals if you were the subject of the investigation?

Administrative and Criminal Investigations – Parallel Lines Do Not Cross[35]

In 1967, The United States Supreme Court (USSC) issued an opinion entitled *Garrity v. State of New Jersey*. The case is perhaps the most important ruling regarding the rights of LEOs. In that case, the Court held that "voluntary" statements obtained from officers who were forced to choose between incriminating themselves in a criminal investigation or losing their jobs were not admissible in a criminal court. Therefore, those statements could not be used against them in a criminal prosecution. The opinion is a great read. You can read the entire opinion on the internet. Just search for *"Garrity v. State of New Jersey."*

The Garrity opinion, as you can imagine, has been studied and examined by courts and agencies all over the United States. Fortunately, the critical points in Garrity hold true today. Those points are based on a few simple principles. First, an agency has an obligation and a right to investigate allegations of misconduct and incidents that involve its LEOs. These *administrative* investigations are focused on clearing officers, determining the effectiveness of policies, and maintaining the integrity of the agency. Second, the agency should be able to compel officers to comply with internal investigations. This principle is based upon the focus of internal investigations as means to evaluate policy, procedure and equipment while determining if a LEO was in compliance with agency policy. Third, a LEO, like any other citizen, has the right to

---

[35] Per the parallel postulate, also called Euclid's fifth postulate because it is the fifth postulate in Euclid's *Elements*. This is a distinctive axiom in Euclidean geometry. You now know all the math I know. Lawyers do not do math, but Sister Imelda would be proud.

remain silent during any *criminal* investigation. As Justice Douglas stated in the opinion, "We conclude that policemen, like teachers and lawyers, are not relegated to a watered-down version of constitutional rights[36]."

In 2010, the Georgia Supreme Court issued an opinion entitled, *State v. Thompson*[37]. Following a shooting, Dekalb County Police Officer Torrey Thompson gave statements to internal affairs investigators and criminal investigators. Prior to the statements and two "walk-throughs" of the scene, supervisors told him he was not permitted to leave the area to avoid the media gathered at the scene. The Georgia Supreme Court held that Officer Thompson's "subjective belief" that he would be punished if he did not cooperate with the criminal investigators was enough for the court to find that his statements to the investigators were NOT voluntary. Therefore, the State could not use those statements against him in the criminal case. It is important to note that Officer Thompson told the court that the agency's policy manual required him to participate in investigations, he was told he was not free to leave, he was *never explicitly told* that he had to cooperate and answer questions, and the criminal and internal affairs investigations were taking place *simultaneously*. The Georgia Supreme Court determined that the trial court must examine the "totality of the circumstances" to decide if the officer had a *reasonable subjective* belief that he was forced to provide the statements at issue. If the officer reasonably believed, based upon the totality of the circumstances, that he was required to answer the questions of the criminal investigators or risk discipline or

---

[36] *Garrity v. State of N.J.*, 385 U.S. 493, 479, 87 S. Ct. 616, 620, 17 L. Ed. 2d 562 (1967)
[37] 288 Ga. 165 (2010)

job loss, those statements cannot be used against the officer in a criminal trial.

So, a few things to consider: Are you familiar with your agency's policies regarding investigations? Are you familiar with and able to articulate the statutes and case law of your state regarding self-defense? Most important, do you still believe you should not have a lawyer present at the scene of a shooting? Are you willing to risk your livelihood and freedom just so you can do it yourself? These are things to think about now...*before* the shooting.

The Role of Counsel

Generally, there is no right to counsel during an administrative investigation. This may not be the case in a state with a Peace Officer's Bill of Rights[38], in an agency which provides a right to counsel, or in an agency with a collective bargaining agreement in place under the Weingarten decision[39]. I have only been excluded from one administrative interview. I must say that this was a silly decision for the law enforcement administrator who excluded me. When you exclude counsel from an administrative interview, you provide her with plenty of ammunition during the appeal process. You and your

---

[38] Nineteen states currently have a Peace Officer's Bill Of Rights that provides specific rights and protection to LEOs who are the subject of investigation. They are: AR(model code available for adoption by local government); AZ; CA; DE; FL; IL; IA; KY; LA; MD; MN; NV; NM; RI; TN; TX; VA; WV; & WI; Eleven states have considered such legislation in the past. They are: CO (2012); HI (2002); KS (1997); MA (1998); MI (2001); MT (1993); ND (2001); PA (2001); SC (1997); UT (1999); WA (1995). Georgia does not currently have such a law as of 2012. Absent civil service or merit system protection, LEOs in Georgia are generally employees at will.

[39] Weingarten provides a right to have a representative present if a member of a collective bargaining unit is subject to investigation. *N.L.R.B. v. Weingarten*, 420 U.S. 251 (1975).

investigators will be forced to admit, under oath at an appeal hearing or in a court, that your agency allows suspects to have counsel, but does not extend the same courtesy to employees.

The role of counsel at an administrative interview is the subject of some controversy. While the courts have consistently permitted counsel to be present at any interview that involves the potential use of the information in a criminal case, the protections afforded under Garrity are a double-edged sword. In an interesting opinion, the Sixth Circuit Federal Court of Appeals held that the right to counsel and the right against self-incrimination *did not* extend to an interview that explicitly was not criminal in nature, even though the investigation had the potential to involve criminal activities. "By its terms, the Fifth Amendment does not prohibit the act of compelling a self-incriminating statement other than for use in a criminal case...The statements given by Officers Lingler and Gezymalla were not used against them in any criminal case. Indeed, under *Garrity v. New Jersey*, 385 U.S. 493, 87 S.Ct. 616, 17 L.Ed.2d 562 (1967), the statements could not have been so used." *Lingler v. Fechko*, 312 F.3d 237, 239 (6th Cir. 2002). You should assume that you have no guaranteed right to counsel in an administrative interview absent a specific policy, state statute or collective bargaining agreement that provides such rights.

While the Garrity Court did not specifically spell out the right to have counsel present or the role of counsel at an administrative interview, the Court did say the following:

The choice given petitioners was either to forfeit their jobs or to incriminate themselves. The option to lose their means of livelihood or to pay the penalty of self-incrimination is the antithesis of free choice to speak out or to remain silent. That practice, like interrogation practices we reviewed in *Miranda v. State of Arizona*, is 'likely to exert such pressure upon an individual as to disable him from making a free and rational choice.' We think the statements were infected by the coercion inherent in this scheme of questioning and cannot be sustained as voluntary under our prior decisions.

Where the choice is 'between the rock and the whirlpool,' duress is inherent in deciding to 'waive' one or the other...'It always is for the interest of a party under duress to choose the lesser of two evils. But the fact that a choice was made according to interest does not exclude duress. It is the characteristic of duress properly so called.'

The question in this case, however, is not cognizable in those terms. Our question is whether a State, contrary to the requirement of the Fourteenth Amendment, can use the threat of discharge to secure incriminatory evidence against an employee.

We held in *Slochower v. Board of Education*, that a public school teacher could not be discharged merely because he had invoked the Fifth Amendment privilege against self-

incrimination when questioned by a congressional committee:

'The privilege against self-incrimination
would be reduced to a hollow mockery if its
exercise could be taken as equivalent either
to a confession of guilt or a conclusive
presumption of perjury...The privilege serves
to protect the innocent who otherwise might
be ensnared by ambiguous circumstances.'

We conclude that policemen, like teachers
and lawyers, are not relegated to a watered-
down version of constitutional rights.

We now hold the protection of the
individual under the Fourteenth Amendment
against coerced statements prohibits use in
subsequent criminal proceedings of statements
obtained under threat of removal from office,
and that it extends to all, whether they are
policemen or other members of our body
politic.

Garrity v. State of New Jersey, 385 U.S. 493,
478 -500(1967). (Internal citations omitted).

It is difficult to read these sections of the Garrity
opinion and conclude that LEOs should not be entitled to
counsel during an administrative interview. However, this
is the current state of the law. In a profession that begins
with an oath to uphold the Constitution of the United
States, it is appalling that some LEOs are not entitled to
have an attorney present during an administrative
interview. After sitting with many LEOs and speaking
with many agency heads, I have yet to hear an intelligent

argument for excluding attorneys at this stage of an investigation.

Keep in mind that Garrity was a plurality opinion, meaning that the Court was divided with five justices voting for the opinion and four dissenting. Essentially, this means the case easily could have been decided against the rights of the LEOs. The bottom line is this: if you want the right to have counsel present during an administrative interview, push for a Peace Officer's Bill of Rights in your state. Policies and agency heads may change, and collective bargaining agreements can expire, but such a law will secure your right to counsel forever.

Garrity was not the last case to address this issue and unfortunately this issue will likely be examined by courts in the future. The USSC revisited this issue again a year later in *Uniformed Sanitation Men Ass'n v. Comm'r of Sanitation of City of New York*, 392 U.S. 280(1968). The Court again reiterated that public employees are entitled to remain silent in the face of a *criminal* investigation. The Court went further, stating that unless the public employee was given clear immunity for statements, the employee could not be compelled to provide testimony, nor could the employee be terminated for failing to do so. The language of this case is very clear and strong:

[The employees] were not discharged merely for refusal to account for their conduct as employees of the city. *They were dismissed for invoking and refusing to waive their constitutional right against self-incrimination.* They were discharged for refusal to expose themselves to criminal prosecution based on testimony which they would give under compulsion, despite their constitutional privilege. Three were asked to sign waivers of immunity before the grand jury. Twelve were told that their answers to questions put to them by the Commissioner of Investigation could be used against them in subsequent proceedings, and were discharged for refusal to answer the questions on this basis. *Garrity v. State of New Jersey*, 385 U.S. 493 (1967), in which we held that testimony compelled by threat of dismissal from employment could not be used in a criminal prosecution of the witness, had not been decided when these 12 petitioners were put to their hazardous choice. In any event, we need not decide whether these petitioners would have effectively waived this constitutional protection if they had testified following the warning that their testimony could be used against them. *They were entitled to remain silent because it was clear that New York was seeking, not merely an accounting of their use or abuse of their public trust, but testimony from their own lips which, despite the constitutional prohibition, could be used to prosecute them criminally. Uniformed Sanitation Men Ass'n v. Comm'r of Sanitation of City of New York*, 392 U.S. 280, 283-84 (1968) (emphasis added).

This case is often overlooked in LEO circles because it does not involve LEOs. However, the case directly addresses the protections afforded public employees of any title. Consider this last quote from the case:

> Petitioners as public employees are entitled, like all other persons, to the benefit of the Constitution, including the privilege against self-incrimination. [citations omitted]. At the same time, petitioners, being public employees, subject themselves to dismissal if they refuse to account for their performance of their public trust, *after proper proceedings, which do not involve an attempt to coerce them to relinquish their constitutional rights. Uniformed Sanitation Men Ass'n v. Comm'r of Sanitation of City of New York*, 392 U.S. 280, 284–85 (1968). (Emphasis added).

The concepts could not be more clear. An administrative investigation must be separate and apart from a criminal investigation and the employee is entitled to a clear expression of immunity from criminal prosecution if he is compelled to testify with an administrative investigation.

In 1973, the United States Court of Claims issued an opinion in the case of *Kalkines v. United States*, 473 F.2d 1391 (Ct. Cl. 1973)(amended on rehearing)[40]. This case is quite instructive and has been cited many times. The case is also

---

[40] The United States Court of Claims was established in 1855 to hear claims against the United States. Opinions were directly appealable to the United States Supreme Court. The court was abolished in 1982 and jurisdiction was transferred to the United States Court of Federal Claims. Appellate jurisdiction for the court now lies with United States Court of Appeals For The Federal Circuit.

an illustration of how administrative investigations can get off-track, how investigators can lose focus, and just how persistent LEOs and their attorneys must be to protect the LEO's constitutional rights. Kalkines worked for the Bureau of Customs. In 1967, he was under investigation for impropriety based upon an allegation that he accepted $200 in exchange for favorable treatment on a customs entry. Kalkines was interviewed on four separate occasions in two states. At some point, he retained an attorney. Over the course of the investigation, he was made aware that criminal charges could arise from the acts alleged against him. He was also advised that these four interviews constituted an administrative investigation. However, Kalkines would not cooperate because he was not provided immunity from prosecution for any statements he made during the administrative investigation or from any information gleaned from his statements. At the end of this process, the agency terminated Kalkines for failing to cooperate with an administrative investigation[41]. He appealed through his agency's appellate procedure and eventually to the United States Court of Claims.

It is important to note that the investigation at issue took place while the Garrity and *Sanitation* cases were being briefed, argued, and decided by the USSC. In short, this was a new area of law. However, what we see in the Kalkines opinion is a clear statement by a federal court of the strength of the constitutional principles at issue.

The Kalkines Court reversed the termination of the employee stating that the employee was clearly and justifiably concerned about a pending criminal investigation and in that investigation, he had a constitutional right to

---

[41] *Kalkines v. United States*, 473 F.2d 1391 (Ct. Cl. 1973) (amended on rehearing)

remain silent. The Court placed the burden *on the agency* to show that Kalkines was clearly told that this was an administrative investigation *and* that he was entitled at all times to immunity for any statements made during that investigation. This was especially true when Kalkines expressed his concern about the nature of the investigation in light of the pending criminal case:

> The agent replied 'that the following interview is administrative in nature, that it is not criminal, that there is no criminal action pending against you and that the purpose of this interview is entirely on an employer-employee basis and that furthermore any answers given to questions put to you in the interview cannot and will not be used against you in any criminal action'[42]; that if the interview were in connection with a criminal action the attorney would most certainly be permitted to be present and to advise; and 'this is an administrative interview and do you understand that this interview is administrative and accordingly your attorney will not be permitted to be present during the interview.' The agent concluded these observations by asking plaintiff whether he would answer questions in counsel's absence.
>
> The defendant urges that this was proper and sufficient advice to Mr. Kalkines that he had immunity against use of his responses.

---

[42] The Court of Claims reviewed the transcripts of the recorded interviews.

But even the agent's most explicit statement was incomplete since it did not refer to the fruits of the answers (in addition to the answers themselves). Moreover, and very significantly, the remainder of the colloquy shows that plaintiff was still very concerned about a criminal prosecution and that the agent never properly brought home that he would have immunity with respect to his answers. *Kalkines v. U.S.*, 473 F.2d 1391, 1396-97 (Ct. Cl. 1973).

Even though the government claimed that these warnings were sufficient, the Court disagreed.

The government in Kalkines also attempted to place the burden on the employee and his attorney to know that immunity was attached to statements made during an administrative investigation. The Court rejected this position:

The Government suggests that Mr. Kalkines, or at least his lawyer, should have known that his answers (and their fruits) could not be used to his disadvantage, and therefore that the explicit caution mandated by *Uniformed Sanitation Men II* might be omitted. *With respect to the plaintiff, a frightened layman, this is certainly an unacceptable position; he could not be expected to know what lawyers and judges were even then arguing about. The case is hardly better for insisting that the attorney should have known, and should have been responsible for alerting his client. Kalkines v. U.S.,* 473 F.2d 1391, 1396 (Ct. Cl. 1973) (emphasis added).

The Court further stated its displeasure with this argument stating as follows:

> Plaintiff was not "duly advised of his options and the consequences of his choice." Quite the opposite, *he was left to squirm with a choice he should not have been put to–the possibility of going to jail or of losing his job. Kalkines v. U.S.,* 473 F.2d 1391, 1395–96 (Ct. Cl. 1973). (Emphasis added).

There can be no doubt that the agency will bear the burden in this area at all times. The same is true in a criminal case where the government must prove that a confession was knowingly and voluntarily[43] provided.

As in every case, the Kalkines Court set forth its reasoning. The opinion sets out the factors that should be considered in this analysis:

> The essential aspects are four: First, in describing a "conduct" investigation the *agent clearly indicated that a criminal investigation or trial was still possible;* he contented himself with reiterating that his own concern was "administrative" and he was not pursuing a violation of criminal law, without denying that a criminal

---

[43] *Miranda v. Arizona,* 384. U.S. 436 (1966); *Dickerson v. US,* 530 U.S. 428 (2000).

proceeding could possibly eventuate. Second, the *agent never really responded to plaintiff's query as to whether the criminal investigation had been dropped, and did not tell him that the U.S. Attorney had refused to go forward with prosecution.* Third, the *agent failed to repeat or even refer to the earlier statement about non-use for criminal purposes of* [Kalkines'] *plaintiff's answers* in this "administrative" inquiry. Fourth, [Kalkines] *was obviously, and quite reasonably, left uncertain as to the connection between the questioning he was then being asked to undergo and a potential criminal action.* This last element seems to us reinforced by some confused remarks of [Kalkines] later on in the exchange–after the agent had commenced to ask specific questions–which seem to express great doubt about the separation between the civil and criminal sides of the investigation. *Kalkines v. U.S.,* 473 F.2d 1391, 1397 (Ct. Cl.1973).

It is interesting that thirty years prior to the decision in *Thompson v. State,* cited earlier, we have an analysis of the subjective beliefs of the LEO as well as the objective analysis of the statements made by the investigators.

So what was the end result? Well, the case did not end well for the agency. The language is worth reading. Here is the exact quote:

...by failing to make and maintain a clear and unequivocal declaration of plaintiff's "use" immunity[44], the customs agents gave the employee very good reason to be apprehensive that he could be walking into the criminal trap if he responded to potentially incriminating questions, and that in that dangerous situation he very much needed his lawyer's help. The record compels this conclusion. Perhaps the agents were not more positive in their statements because there still remained at that time the possibility of prosecution. Whatever the basis for their failure to clear up plaintiff's reasonable doubts, we are convinced the record shows that he was not 'duly advised of his options and the consequences of his choice.' His failure to respond was excused on this occasion, as on the earlier dates cited in the other specifications. The agency and the Civil Service Commission erred in disregarding this justification and in holding that the duty to respond was absolute and was violated.

The *result is that, for this reason, plaintiff's discharge in 1968 was invalid, and he is now entitled to recover his lost pay, less offsets.*

---

[44] "immunity...may be "transactional," which protects the person testifying against prosecution for any transaction touched on in his testimony whether or not his involvement can be independently proven. A more limited immunity, "use and derivative use" immunity, protects the witness from the use of either the incriminating testimony or the fruits of such testimony." *State v. Hanson*, 249 Ga. 739, 741, 295 S.E.2d 297, 300 (1982).

Kalkines v. U.S., 473 F.2d 1391, 1398 (Ct. Cl. 1973). (Emphasis added).

Kalkines is a great case to illustrate the points in this chapter. This is especially true in this last quote that outlines the use of and value of statements improperly solicited during an administrative interview, as well as the authority of an agency to terminate a LEO who refuses to comply with an administrative investigation after properly being properly advised of his rights.

> It is now settled that the individual cannot be discharged simply because he invokes his Fifth Amendment privilege against self-incrimination in refusing to respond. Conversely, a later prosecution cannot constitutionally use statements (or their fruits) coerced from the employee–in an earlier disciplinary investigation or proceeding–by a threat of removal from office if he fails to answer the question. But *a governmental employer is not wholly barred from insisting that relevant information be given it; the public servant can be removed for not replying if he is adequately informed both that he is subject to discharge for not answering and that his replies (and their fruits) cannot be employed against him in a criminal case.* *Kalkines v. U.S.*, 473 F.2d 1391, 1393 (Ct. Cl. 1973). (Emphasis added).

This principle has been upheld and expanded. With the immunity from prosecution comes the requirement to cooperate or face termination[45].

Citizen Review Panels

Although not prevalent across the United States, some jurisdictions have adopted a program to have panels of civilians review use of force incidents. An internet search for such programs yields thousands of hits.

The panels are usually established in response to an actual or perceived rise in use of force or abuse of authority incidents by LEOs[46]. The members of such panels include community leaders, politicians, media, and advocates. The public sentiment is, as expected, sharply divided about the need for and the propriety of such review panels. However, the concept is firmly established in the United States. In fact, in 1995, the National Association for Civilian Oversight of Law Enforcement (NACOLE[47]) was established in Maryland and is currently based in Indiana. According to their website, their mission is as follows:

---

[45] Accordingly, we hold that a police officer may be dismissed for just cause within the meaning of R.C. 4141.29(D)(2)(a) when he or she refuses to obey a superior's reasonable order to take a polygraph test, so long as the officer has been informed as part of such order (1) of the subject of the intended inquiry, which is specifically and narrowly related to the performance of the officer's official duties, (2) that the officer's answers cannot be used against him or her in any subsequent criminal prosecution, and (3) that the penalty for such is dismissal. *City of Warrensville Heights v. Jennings*, 569 N.E.2d 489, 494 (OH 1991).

[46] The Atlanta Citizen Review Board was established in 2006 in response to the shooting of ninety-two year old Kathryn Johnston. The Board has publicly sought subpoena power because officers have refused to appear or testify when they did appear.

[47] www.nacole.org

...a non-profit organization that brings together individuals and agencies working to establish or improve oversight of police officers in the United States. NACOLE welcomes people and organizations committed to fair and professional law enforcement that is responsive to community needs.

NACOLE is dedicated to promoting greater police accountability through the establishment or improvement of citizen oversight agencies by

- Organizing an annual training conference to increase the knowledge and skills of staff members and volunteers who work in oversight.
- Providing technical assistance and advice to jurisdictions that are considering the creation or revitalization of oversight bodies.
- Identifying best practices as they emerge from the experiences of members.
- Encouraging networking, communication and information-sharing to counter the isolation inherent in the profession.
- Furnishing information to government officials and community representatives that will support their advocacy of oversight in their states, counties, cities, and towns.

The group holds an annual conference, provides mentoring, training, and certification to members who wish to become involved in police oversight groups, and provides resources and materials to members.

Citizen oversight panels, which exist in many forms, can work with police agencies to improve community relations and provide insight for police administrators. For example, at least one study published online deals with LEO fatigue and its effect on safety of officers and citizens. However, their role in the administrative handling of a use of force incident raises many questions such as:

1. Does the panel have the power to subpoena the LEO to provide testimony?
2. Is the LEO entitled to refuse to testify?
3. Is the LEO entitled to counsel if she does appear?
4. Are statements made to such a panel afforded protection under *Garrity v. NJ*[48]?
5. Will LEOs be subject to discipline if they refuse to appear?

As predicted, these concerns have led to mini standoffs between the panels, the government, and the agency. Unfortunately, in my opinion, the LEOs are left in the middle of the dispute.

For what it's worth, my opinion on these panels is simple. Like the overwhelming majority of LEOs, I welcome suggestions, review of procedures, community involvement, and support. I have no concern with a panel

---

[48] 385 U.S. 493 (1967).

that seeks to review public documents, provide input regarding police practices, and provide a forum for open dialogue between the agency and the community. However, there are numerous provisions in law enforcement to allow for oversight of the actions of LEOs including, but not limited to, certification on a state and national level by independent agencies, investigations by state and federal agencies, multi-jurisdictional shoot teams, and grand juries to review the actions of LEOs. It is amazing to me that citizen review committees seek to review the actions of LEOs to a degree that requires live testimony. No other profession would be subject to such review. Imagine a citizen review panel to study accounting done by financial analysts for a city, or a panel to review the litigation strategy of a county attorney's office. The public would not stand for that and there is a public recognition that a group of untrained persons on a panel would not be qualified to engage in such activities.

As a profession, we need to do a better job of communicating our procedures for investigating use of force incidents and allegations of misconduct. I am convinced that LEOs effectively regulate the conduct of their own, more so than any other profession. However, perception is reality. We have the obligation to influence the perception that we are unable to "police" our own. If we do not control the message, someone else will.

Mutual Aid and
Multi-Jurisdictional Law Enforcement Units

Multi-jursdictional law enforcement units are not a new concept. Their origins can be traced to federal grant programs, efforts to address specific crimes on a regional basis, and crime sprees that necessitated the joint efforts of multiple law enforcement agencies. The United States Department of Justice defines such units as:

> A MJTF (Multi-Jurisdictional Task Force) is a cooperative law enforcement effort involving two or more criminal justice agencies, with jurisdiction over two or more areas, sharing the common goal of addressing drug control or violent crime problems. MJTFs allow law enforcement agencies in different jurisdictions to work together as a single enforcement entity with the ability to improve communication, share intelligence, and coordinate activities. This allows for more efficient use of resources and targeting of offenders whose activities cross jurisdictional boundaries[49].

Currently, units exist to address a plethora of criminal activity including money laundering, terrorism, child exploitation, human trafficking, gang activity, fraud, terrorism, and illegal immigration. The United States Department of Justice maintains training and evaluation programs to increase the effectiveness of these units. Curiously absent from the criteria is any reflection of how individual members of the unit will be treated following a use of force incident or how the agencies commit to the resolution of administrative conflicts that arise from the

---

[49] http://www.ojp.usdoj.gov/BJA/evaluation/program-law-enforcement/forces1.htm

presence of LEOs from several jurisdictions working together.

The prevalence of these units cannot be overlooked. For example, St. Petersburg College in Florida has a program specifically designed to teach how to set up and run such units. The website for the program, run in cooperation with the Florida National Guard, is www.mctft.com. Here is an excerpt from their website:

The **Multijurisdictional Counterdrug Task Force Training (MCTFT)** program provides unique, tuition-free, courses covering all aspects of counterdrug law enforcement and training support for community anti-drug coalitions. The program is a federally funded partnership through the Department of Defense between the Florida National Guard and St. Petersburg College. The program is nationally responsive and is located at the Southeastern Public Safety Institute (SEPSI) of St. Petersburg College in St. Petersburg, Florida. SEPSI is a state-of-the-art facility with a wide variety of special features to enhance the training received. In all courses, the safety of law enforcement, military, and civilian lives is of paramount importance.

Since its inception in 1993, MCTFT has trained more than 1,000,000 students throughout the 50 states and four U.S. territories by instructor-led classes, satellite-based training programs, CD-ROM independent study courses, and online eDrug training courses. MCTFT employs over 250 professional trainers, coordinators and staff at the Center for Public Safety Innovation (CPSI) site in St. Petersburg, Florida. In addition, MCTFT partners with local, state, and federal organizations to strengthen our ability to provide the highest quality training available today.

In 2003, the State of Illinois alone boasted twenty-one such units that focused upon drug interdiction[50]. Many, if not most, units are established and maintained through the use of grants including the Byrne Fund[51]. After 9-11, the United States Department of Justice Bureau of Justice Assistance (USDOJBJA) renewed efforts to establish such units and advocated for the enhanced use of the concept to combat domestic and international terrorism. Finally, the USDOJBJA currently advocates expanding the concept to mutual aid for emergencies[52].

Traditionally, mutual aid agreements have been used on a limited basis to organize investigative teams or task forces. Today, these agreements are being used regionally to address the threats of international and domestic terrorism as agencies recognize

---

[50] Illinois Criminal Justice Information Authority, *On Good Authority*, Vol. 6, No. 6 "A comparison of local and multi-jurisdictional drug enforcement efforts in Illinois." Feb. 2003.
[51] Edward Byrne Memorial Justice Assistance Grant (JAG) Program is administered by the U.S. Department of Justice, Bureau of Justice Assistance (BJA)
[52] Mutual Aid: Multijurisdictional Partnerships for Meeting Regional Threats Sept. 2005 Publication No. NCJ 210679

that a more collaborative approach is necessary to prevent future attacks against our communities. Moreover, regional mutual aid agreements can be tailored to meet specific needs, address likely threats, and make available the full range of existing resources that can be brought to bear quickly in times of emergency.

In short, these units are here to stay and will become more prevalent in the future.

Typically, these units incorporate city, county, state and federal agencies. Each has its own policies and procedures that guide its activities. Although the units are evaluated across a complicated matrix for effectiveness, fiscal responsibility, and use of grant resources, there is virtually no effort spent to reconcile the policies and procedures applicable to the LEOs who comprise the working members of the task force. While no one can dispute the effectiveness of these units, what happens when the LEOs involved in the unit have a need for representation and those rules do not align? This is especially true when dealing with officer involved shootings or discipline. While most state and local jurisdictions require LEOs to comply with internal and criminal investigations, most federal agencies will not allow their agents to submit to questioning by local administrative investigators or criminal investigators. This divergence also arises with regard to disability and line of duty death benefits.

For example, Clay Strayhorn, one of my firm's associate attorneys, served on a rapid-entry, high-risk search warrant service comprised of agents from two federal law enforcement agencies, one state agency, and four local agencies. On one occasion, they had a briefing about the evidence and people they were looking for, the location of the closest hospital if things went badly, and the following use of force instructions: "Go by your agency's use of force policy." There were seven use of force policies in play on that raid, and none of the agents knew anything about policies of the other agencies. Fortunately, everything went smoothly.

Several years ago, I represented two county sheriff deputies who were involved in a shooting while working for a fugitive task force. The task force contained members of city, state, military, and federal jurisdictions. Not surprisingly, the task force was spearheaded by the United States Marshals Service. Although several officers fired at the suspect, I represented the deputy with the best marksmanship. The suspect, who feigned having a weapon, was unarmed and died from his injuries. Throughout the investigation and the "special investigative grand jury," convened to look at use of force incidents, we ran into difficulty. While the state and local jurisdictions cooperated in every way with the administrative and criminal investigations, the federal agencies refused to do so. They refused to provide statements, reports, or the intelligence about the criminal history of the suspect who caused the LEOs to approach the apartment with a body bunker and ultimately shoot him[53]. To this day, the file of the agency that worked the homicide is incomplete.

When examining any situation involving multi-jurisdictional units, you should start with the Memorandum

---

[53] The intelligence disseminated in a pre-raid briefing explained that the suspect was armed, his co-conspirators were in custody, he was a suspect in homicides and armed robberies, and he was in possession of several weapons and body armor when he was previously arrested.

of Understanding (MOU) drafted when the unit began. The MOU covers many issues. However, you will find a paucity of information regarding which agency's policy applies in a given situation. Another resource is the enabling legislation that preceded or authorized the creation of the unit. An example of such legislation is found in Georgia law at O.C.G.A. § 36-69-3.1:

> Any county or municipality in this state shall be authorized to enter into contracts and mutual aid agreements with counties or municipalities of any other state or with any agency of the United States for the provision of law enforcement services in a local emergency to the extent that the laws of such other state or the United States permit such joint contracts or agreements to furnish one another assistance in law enforcement. Any such contract or mutual aid agreement shall have incorporated therein the provisions of Code Sections 36-69-4 through 36-69-8. Any such contract or mutual aid agreement entered into by a county shall not become effective until approved by the sheriff of such county.

A review of enabling legislation in several states indicates that this Georgia statute is fairly generic. Finally, most units utilize oversight by a group of agency heads. All department heads should encourage coordination between agencies *prior* to a critical incident.

Of course these issues become more clear under a collective bargaining agreement. The rights of the LEO stem from state law and the contract. I would argue for the inclusion of rights for any issues unique to these units in any collective bargaining agreement. This is especially true as the LEOs may be far from their jurisdiction and representatives when an OIS occurs.

So here is the takeaway for your attorney and points for LEOs to keep in mind when dealing with multi-jurisdictional task forces or mutual aid situations as a LEO working on in this environment, an agency head involved in such a group or as counsel for LEOs:

1. Read the MOU to know who the players are.

2. Use the MOU to make policy arguments that help your employees or client. For example, can you argue additional rights if your city LEO is serving as a sworn federal officer at the time of the incident?

3. Know the enabling legislation and determine ASAP whether the unit was properly established.

4. Use the chain of command within the unit when evaluating disciplinary issues. For example, a direct order from a supervisor within the unit may conflict with department policy, but be entirely consistent with the policy within the unit.

5. When small issues arise, take the opportunity to prepare for the big ones. For example, a minor car wreck and foot chase may flush

out conflicting policies and procedures. It is best to take the time to work through those conflicts while the stakes are low.

6. Remember that nearly all of these units are funded, at least partially, by federal and state grants. Within those grants, you may find reporting requirements that outline more clearly the unique obligations of members of the unit.

7. Meet with counsel for the LEOs of the agencies that comprise the units. Roundtable these issues before the subpoenas are served. In the example I used above, I was able to get the attorney for the federal officers to provide enough intelligence to clear my client.

8. Recognize that there is always a good faith argument that a LEO will be subject to the policy of his agency irrespective of any conflicting policies of the unit.

9. Realize that LEOs who work in these units rarely want to leave. These are coveted positions and LEOs may not want to make waves to fight disciplinary issues.

10. Realize that any allegation of wrongdoing within the unit will likely escalate to the USDOJ quickly.

CHAPTER SIX
THE MEDIA INVESTIGATION

I keep telling my wife not to watch the news or read the paper, but she wants to know what is happening then she gets real upset when she finds out what people are saying. I understand because I read one article and I got really upset.

–Name withheld

"Here now, the news." The phrase made famous by Roger Grimsby and later parodied by Chevy Chase leads me to the topic of this chapter. The role of the media is as entrenched in our country as freedom itself. I personally believe the order of the Constitutional Amendments found in the Bill of Rights is rational, rather than random. The freedom of the press is guaranteed on the same level as freedom of religion and the freedom to petition the government for a redress of grievance[54]. Therefore, no one should be surprised that journalists take their profession[55] and their roles in society seriously.

So, what is the role of the media after a critical incident? First, you should expect inquiries into the facts. This is the core function of the media: Inquire. Second, it is reasonable to expect resistance to any perceived or actual restrictions on information. This is the second function of the media: Be steadfast in the pursuit of the facts. Third, expect skepticism. This is yet another function of the media: Stay objective and avoid bias. In short, the media will cover the incident, the investigative process, the outcome of the investigations, and the reaction of the public. Their involvement will typically begin with a response to the scene.

Joe Friday's iconic statement, "just the facts ma'am," has become the mantra all too often of Public Information Officers (PIOs) and law enforcement administrators, as well as the attorneys who defend law enforcement agencies. Many LEOs have finally come to grips with the fact that the media is everywhere. Twenty-five years ago,

---

[54] It is also not surprising that the Second Amendment guaranteed the private right to keep and bear arms. *District of Columbia v. Heller*, 554 U.S. 570(2008).
[55] I have always been amazed at the strange dichotomy between LEOs and journalists. While both professions are committed to the truth, only the former takes an oath.

the "media" consisted of a mainstream media dominated by print, radio, and television. Today, with the advent of social media, cell phone cameras, and the near complete proliferation of surveillance, traffic, and dash cams in law enforcement vehicles in the United States, there is no shortage of "media" available following a critical incident. The Federal Freedom of Information Act (FOIA) and similar state statutes provide professional journalists, amateur journalists, and the average citizen with an endless supply of video, audio, and written documentation of the actions of LEOs all around the United States and the world.

I am a staunch defender of the First Amendment to the Constitution of the United States. In fact, you will find that I am a staunch defender of the entire Constitution, including the Second Amendment, the Sixth Amendment, and everything that provides due process to LEOs. So, in this chapter you will not hear me rail about the evils of access to law enforcement files, videos, audio-taped interviews of suspects, and the like. Instead, my perspective is a bit different. Due to today's relative ease of access to what was once hard-to-reach sensitive law enforcement information, a PIO, law enforcement administrator, or LEO who steps into the arena of the media frenzy following a critical incident enters a coliseum with very different rules. Compared to twenty-five years ago, the number of spectators has increased, and so has the number of lions. Just like any other game, when the rules change, you have to change the playbook. This chapter will explore some strategies for handling inquiries from the media and the public following your next critical incident. We will explore some of the mine fields for officers handling media inquiries on a regular basis and also explore the effect of an agency's media response on future litigation. Hopefully, by the end of the chapter, you will consider these options as groundwork for the future defense of a civil suit, criminal action, or just a publicity inquiry concerning the actions of your agency.

In my experience, most members of the media are professionals. They take their jobs seriously and pride themselves on the legacy of a profession practiced by many patriots throughout history. This is not to say that I have never disagreed or had spirited discussions with members of the media. Dissent and disagreement are the cornerstones of human interaction, professional relationships and democracy. LEOs certainly rely on the media to assist with calls for victims and witnesses, as well as to broadcast proactive efforts to prevent crime. In turn, the media relies upon LEOs to help them investigate and report.

The Rise of the "Informal Media"

In our internet-driven world, the most important thing to remember is the role of the "informal media," which is my name for the unofficial "reporting" on the internet. This includes blogs, social media sites, on-line only news sites, and the comment section of on-line news sources. The concern for LEOs and agencies is the speed with which the informal media will respond with postings about a critical incident. Although some bloggers are professional journalists, unlike the media professionals described above, often this "reporting" is no more than the promulgation of conjecture and bias in furtherance of an agenda. The fairly new practice of allowing people to anonymously comment on news stories contained on legitimate internet news sites has, in my humble opinion, led to a blurring of the lines between media professionals who researched the story and people merely advancing an agenda. I challenge you to search a few recent officer involved shootings to get a glimpse of this phenomenon.

So, how can LEOs and agencies prepare for the response of the media, formal and informal, to a critical incident? First, recognize that you must prepare for and respond to media inquiries. Second, you must use the internet as a vehicle for your response and take proactive steps, such as posting press releases on your agency's webpage and social media accounts to get your agency's word out. You cannot afford to let those with ulterior motives get ahead of you in cyberspace.

Control the Dialogue and Fix Erroneous Public Perceptions

The call came in as a "trouble unknown" call. Two units responded to the Gas-Mart at the corner of 5th and Elm. Knowing this was not a low crime area, both LEOs were on alert, and appropriately poised for anything that can arise when responding to a trouble unknown call. The LEOs arrived to see the parking lot packed with people buying gas, talking to each other, and entering and leaving the parking lot. They approached the building from side entrances, seeking to avoid a hostage situation in case the trouble unknown call was actually an armed robbery in progress. They began making an effort to look inside the store. However, despite the best efforts of the agency's Crime Prevention Unit over the past several years, the owner of the store had plastered the windows with advertisements and signs that prevented the LEOs from seeing inside of the store. Because of this, there was no way for the LEOs to determine what was happening inside the store without exposing themselves to a threat inside. As they watched the business for approximately a minute, they noticed that no one was exiting the store. Obviously, this was a bad sign. One LEO instructed dispatch to contact the store and determine more information about what was going on. Dispatch reluctantly told the LEOs they were unable to make contact inside.

Other units were on the way and the LEOs were attempting to set up a perimeter when a customer exited the store. The customer appeared calm and the LEOs waited until he turned the corner to ask him what was going on inside. The customer stated, "There's some guy in there raising hell. I don't know what his problem is. He's not wearing a shirt. He is yelling, but I can't understand him. I guess he's drunk. The staff is trying to calm him down. I just left a ten dollar bill on the counter for a seven dollar six pack and walked out." The LEOs quickly got his name and advised radio what they had learned. They formulated a plan and prepared to make entry into the building as other units arrived.

As the door swung open a couple of seconds later, they made a concerted effort to enter the building at that time to avoid any further disturbance to anything going on inside. As they entered the business, both LEOs saw two employees in Gas-Mart shirts. They were clearly agitated and scared and were hiding behind the register. Two or three patrons were up against one of the walls afraid to pass near a suspect who was standing at the open cooler where single drinks and alcoholic beverages are dispensed. The LEOs split up so they were not standing next to each other. One LEO went to the left to outflank the individual and one stood closer to the counter to provide protection for the patrons and the employees in case things went bad. The officer, who made the turn to the left, quietly provided dispatch with a description of the suspect and provided more information to responding units.

Upon walking up to the counter, the LEO asked one of the employees to go open the back door for responding units. His intent was to gain more entry points for the building without agitating the suspect. However, in his mind, he could not imagine a more agitated suspect. With fifteen years of experience, ten of which were spent as a field training officer, the LEO was no stranger to agitated suspects or emotionally disturbed persons. However, something here was different. Put simply, this suspect was enormous. The LEO would later estimate his weight at well beyond 300 pounds and his height at six feet five inches. Although it was only thirty-five degrees outside, the suspect was barefoot, wearing a pair of shorts, and shirtless. His chest showed signs that he had been in some sort of a scuffle, as he had fingernail marks across his chest. He reeked of alcohol, and the words he was yelling were clearly slurred. The suspect was holding a quart beer bottle in each hand. He was apparently staring at the cooler as if trying to resolve some sort of question in his mind. When the LEOs came in, their tactic of waiting for the door to open prior to making entry worked. The suspect was initially unaware of their presence. However, he looked up, saw the uniform, and fixated on the LEO.

The LEO would later recount that the stare from the suspect was penetrating and cold. "He seemed to be looking at and through me." Realizing that there were backup units on the way and a partner inside the business, the LEO began to speak to the suspect in very calming tones, opening his palms to try to ease the suspect's agitation. While initially this tactic appeared to be working, the suspect suddenly exploded from his location and attacked the LEO. When questioned, the remaining clerk behind the counter described the suspect taking a few steps and then jumping nearly ten feet, landing on the LEO. Although the LEO attempted to move laterally out of the way of the big man, the suspect landed on him with full force. The LEO attempted to push him off to gain some distance for a tactical advantage. However, the suspect struck the LEO one time with his right forearm and then began an immediate, concerted effort to remove the LEO's firearm from its holster. Predictably, the LEO on the ground made his sole mission his effort to protect his firearm from leaving the holster. However, the large suspect was too strong for his efforts. Just as the LEO believed he was about to get control of the weapon, the suspect started pulling again, nearly lifting him off of the floor. As the LEO felt the holster start to give and the suspect remove the weapon from the holster, the suspect's body suddenly became rigid. Although the weight of the suspect was still on the LEO, he was no longer attempting to remove the weapon and was, in fact, not even struggling or striking the LEO. It took a few seconds for the LEO to realize that his partner was able to maneuver around the suspect and deploy his TASER. Unfortunately, the five second TASER cycle did not provide sufficient time for the LEO on the ground to secure handcuffs on the suspect. As the suspect began to struggle with the LEO again, the backup LEO again deployed the TASER for another five second cycle. This time, expecting the TASER cycle, the LEO on the ground was able to wrestle himself from underneath the suspect and begin to get his handcuffs out. He could also hear sirens from responding units. During the fourth TASER cycle, patrol cars were pulling into the parking lot, LEOs were entering into the front and back doors of the business, and the suspect was finally secured by a third LEO who entered the building. The LEOs called for emergency responders to arrive and treat the suspect and called for a supervisor due to the injuries to the LEO and the suspect. The suspect was transported to the hospital, but not before a local news crew arrived on the scene.

That evening on the news, you hear that the media determined the suspect walked away from a local home for individuals with mental disabilities. He was off of his medication, had threatened to injure several workers at the facility and had actually been in a physical confrontation with one of the other residents. This explained the scratches across his chest. Just as you are listening to the story realizing that the LEOs probably averted a more serious injury to the staff and patrons of the store, you hear the words that send a chill through your spine, "Local law enforcement today tased a mentally disabled man while he looked through a cooler for cold drinks at a grocery store. The man was transported to the hospital with injuries from the struggle and to be evaluated after being tased several times. The LEOs were not injured in the confrontation." Your phone is ringing off the hook. The PIO is wondering what information should be put out, and so another controversy about a lawful use of force begins.

Use the Facts, the Facts Will Set You Free

Faced with the situation described herein, most agencies would put out a press release advising that the LEOs were forced to use a TASER and start immediately defending the LEOs' actions from the perspective of the media and laypeople who know absolutely nothing about the laws surrounding the use of force. Phrases like "the officers had no choice" or "the matter is under investigation" just fuel the fire that the LEOs' actions are subject to review and the agency is concerned. Although some who teach public information classes agree that you should release very little information and state that an investigation is ongoing, I could not disagree more.

In the following weeks, all of you know what will happen. The LEOs' actions will be questioned in the media as to why they did not have any video of the deployment of the TASER or of their approach to the building. They will now be in a position of defending their actions because the agency did not proactively explain why the LEOs made sound tactical decisions. Further, the private company that owns the Gas-Mart, concerned about bad publicity, is very likely to release the surveillance video from the store. A video of a violent encounter with a LEO that is not put in context usually will be misinterpreted. So, given the scenario above, I suggest this press release instead:

> This afternoon, two of our officers responded to a trouble unknown call at the Gas-Mart on Elm Street. Due to the nature of the call, the officers were unable to park in front of the business and had to approach the call as a possible armed robbery in progress. As the officers got closer to the business, they were unable to see into the business due to signs and posters that were placed over the windows by the store owner. When the officers were able to make contact with one of the patrons, they learned that an individual was becoming violent inside the store. As they entered the

store, they could tell that the employees were scared, as were the two patrons inside the business.

When the officers first saw the subject, he was standing at a cooler of drinks with a quart-size glass beer bottle in each hand and was staring and mumbling. The officer, a fifteen year veteran of the force with ten years of experience training other officers, approached the subject in a calm voice attempting to ease his agitation and determine a way to defuse the situation. Unfortunately, the subject immediately attacked the officer, striking him with his elbow. The suspect then began a violent effort to disarm the officer by trying to remove his firearm from the holster. The subject, who was more than six feet five inches tall and weighed more than 300 pounds, was lying on top of the officer trying to jerk his weapon out of his holster. At times, he was picking the officer up off of the floor by his holster as the officer desperately tried to hold onto his firearm. Fortunately, the backup officer was able to deploy a TASER and avoid the use of deadly force against the subject. Due to the subject's continued struggling, and the fact that the subject was still laying on top of the first officer, the backup officer was required to deploy his TASER more than once, in fact a total of four times, and the subject was placed into custody without any further injury. While this was a sad situation in which a person with mental difficulties had a violent encounter with the police, fortunately higher levels of force were averted through the use of proper tactics, training, and the deployment of a less-lethal device known as a TASER.

Aside from the obvious advantage of the publicity, this statement will be used and will assist you when someone is considering whether to sue your agency. An agency that proactively puts out the facts and states in plain terms what happened, along with stating unapologetically exactly what level of force was used, why the force was used, and the injuries suffered by the suspect and the LEOs, I believe is less likely to face a lawsuit and more able to defend a lawsuit should one occur.

You should never miss an opportunity to educate the public, the media, and anyone else who will listen about the laws governing the use of force and the realities facing LEOs on the street.

Other Rules Have Changed As Well

In 2011 and its five preceding years, we saw multiple violent attacks on LEOs. LEOs can now see videos on the internet of other LEOs being attacked. Attacks against LEOs are becoming more prevalent and more violent. Although we can debate the reasons, I personally believe it is because we are letting more and more violent people out of prison, or letting them avoid jail sentences altogether in order to save money. Serial felony offenders are being released from prison, and it is no surprise that many of them recidivate to their violent ways. In addition, LEOs are able to see the dash cameras from other LEOs who were injured or lost their lives on TV and multimedia websites. It is no wonder that LEOs, faced with an increasing violent opposition, are reacting more quickly. It's simply a matter of self-preservation. However, we can use these videos of officers being hurt or killed to our advantage. We use them in training; why not train the public? When the public understands just how quickly a situation on a traffic stop can become deadly, the public will, in my experience, better understand why the LEO used the level of force he chose. When the public understands the level of force used and what the LEO perceived, the public overwhelmingly supports the use of force by LEOs. While there are some who will never support any use of force under any circumstances by LEOs, they are not your audience. You will never change their minds, and they will never understand.

So, here is the takeaway: When you have a critical incident, or any incident in which you know media attention will follow, put the information out there first. Use only the facts that you can back up, verify, and defend in court. Utilize websites and social media to let the public know that you are acting in an open and honest manner. When you have a situation in which a LEO is assaulted, tell the public about it. When you have a situation in which your LEOs had no other options but to use force, state the level of force used, the reason, and the injury to the suspect, *as well as the injury to the LEO*. Do not apologize for the lawful use of force. This is especially true when you have an agency filled with highly trained, highly experienced, and highly professional LEOs. I do not apologize for any efforts that my clients have taken to protect themselves or the lives of another, and neither should you.

Each critical incident and each use of force, especially deadly force, must be examined separately. While law enforcement agencies have the responsibility to disseminate information to the media and the public, the media professionals have the responsibility to fairly report *all* of the facts. When both professions meet their obligations, the public wins.

Going forward, we must be more proactive to control the messages sent through the media. Too often, we are so concerned with the inevitable civil suit following a critical incident that we fail to present the facts. In the world of media, if you do not control the message, someone else will frame the story.

As an example, TASER International recently began keeping statistics on a new category of TASER deployment to document the number of incidents in which deadly force was not needed due to the deployment of the TASER. This is information that must be made available to the public and specifically the media.

Another way to educate the media and the public about the nature of use of force is to change the manner in which we release information on critical incidents. Typically, the PIO or agency head will make a vague statement that includes (1) the actions of the LEO, (2) a statement that the LEO has been placed on administrative leave, and (3) the condition of the suspect. I submit that such statements only fuel the suspicion that the LEO may have acted improperly. I suggest the following types of statements be included in the initial press release or statement:

"The officer was attacked when he arrived on the scene."

"Fortunately, the officer was able to deploy a less than lethal force option, in this case a TASER, and avoid the use of deadly force—quite possibly saving the suspect's life."

"The deputy was in uniform displaying his badge of office when the suspect refused his commands to stop resisting arrest."

"Officers have responded to this address several times in the past year and made arrests for family violence."

"Based upon reports that are available to the public, the suspect has been arrested in the past for crimes of violence."

"The suspect was repeatedly told he was under arrest and continued to resist and fight the officers."

"The deputy's uniform showed clear signs of a struggle and he is being evaluated and treated for his injuries."

Incorporating these types of proactive statements will change the public discourse and prevent the agency and the LEO from fighting conceptions of wrongdoing until the investigations are concluded several weeks or months later.

By changing the tide of negative publicity, negative inferences, and a general suspicion of the use of force, we educate the public and turn the conversations from what the LEOs did wrong to "Why did the suspect take the actions he took?" and "Fortunately, the LEO was able to avoid taking a life." We all know that every physical confrontation with a LEO has the potential to turn deadly. When they do not turn deadly, we should take pride in that fact and let the public know. Further, consider the sheer volume of citizen contacts and confrontations a LEO has over the course of a career, and compare that number of contacts with the fact that the average LEO is involved in only one or two serious use of force or use of deadly force incidents in a twenty year career. Those statistics speak for themselves and help you defend the LEO as a person who judiciously uses force in a reasonable manner, rather than someone who uses excessive force.

As a matter of course, I encourage my clients who are involved in critical incidents to avoid the news coverage and the informal media. I encourage any readers of this book to follow the same policy after being involved in a critical incident or counseling a LEO who has been. You already know what happened—you were there. The inaccuracies, whether honest or intentional, will only serve to upset you as you work through the incident. Any effort to combat these posts on your own will lead to disaster. LEOs have, in the past, attempted to do so anonymously. Without exception, the media and others will determine your identity and this will affect your credibility. In addition, you could find yourself in violation of agency policy for sharing facts and information about an ongoing investigation. Focus instead on your family and your role in the investigation of that incident.

In the end analysis, I would never replace the free press in the United States. It is one of the hallmarks of our democracy. The more we are able to recognize the separate and distinct roles of the media and law enforcement, the more we can safeguard the integrity of our legal system. My biggest fear is that the informal media, aided—albeit unwillingly—by anonymous comment postings to legitimate news stories, will one day compromise the ability of our legal system to analyze the use of force by LEOs. After all, grand juries and trial juries are composed of citizens who read both the well-investigated news stories and off-the-cuff drivel often in the same sitting.

CHAPTER SEVEN
THE CIVIL SIDE OF CRITICAL INCIDENTS

Q: Where were you when you got served?

A: At work. And I got even more upset as I read the suit and allegations in the suit. I was good in my mind of what happened because I know what happened, and you know he tried to kill me. I mean the bottom line was he tried to kill me, and for him getting away was more important than anything.[T]he allegations in the lawsuit were just so out there.

–Name withheld

Why do people file lawsuits? Okay, Okay. You probably think you know the answer to this one: Money! However, that is not always the case. People file lawsuits for many reasons. For instance, I defend a lot of suits by inmates. In many of those cases, they have little else to do. While some people file lawsuits with the hope of compensation, some are looking for answers. Others are looking to make changes. Remember that the filing of a lawsuit does not mean that you did anything improper. Stay focused on your job and staying safe. Let the lawyers handle the details.

It is important to understand these motivations and emotions. This is the reality of a lawsuit. Like any other encounter in life and on the street, you must understand the mindset of your opponent. Readers of this book and my blog comprise LEOs at every level of city, county, state, and federal government, so you are no strangers to lawsuits. In fact, you probably personally know a LEO who has been sued. Maybe you have been sued. In order to understand why people sue LEOs, you must first acknowledge the role of law enforcement in society.

LEOs deal with a varied and somewhat strange sample of society. We bring EMS to the scene and render first aid to the homeless guy who people stepped over for hours. We arrest the millionaire for DUI. We respond to domestic disputes, look for lost children, and seize the assets of criminals of every sort. In short, we see people at their worst or under the worst circumstances. When LEOs show up, people are generally not happy. When they look back upon those interactions, their perceptions are distorted, they often have unresolved issues, and they associate the negative effects of those episodes with LEOs. This explains why the lawsuit often has little to do with the facts, and the statements of the plaintiffs do not match the official LEO report.

In that regard, the people who file lawsuits are no different from many injured people who file suits. I have been honored to represent many injured parties in civil suits, many of whom were LEOs. Many times, we are able to recover large settlements for these people, including settlements exceeding $2,000,000. However, the memory of the event and the aftermath will always cloud the security afforded by a settlement. The tough part about these cases is that many LEOs will forever associate their involvement with the civil process, my office, and me with the worst events of their lives. This is a fact I accept and understand. While the overwhelming majority of LEOs I represent become lifetime friends, some prefer to remain distant. The same is true for LEOs we represent in administrative or licensing issues.

Make no mistake—some people sue for money in the hopes of a quick settlement. Some people sue because they truly believe they were harmed. Others sue to "change the system." Still others sue to find out more about the event that led to an outcome they neither predicted nor intended. This is especially true when an OIS ends in the death of the suspect.

Lawsuits that follow the death of a suspect resulting from an OIS are particularly difficult. The lawsuit must be filed and pursued by a representative of the estate of the deceased person. That person could be a spouse, a sibling, or a parent. They are suing for money damages on behalf of the estate and sometimes for survivor benefits. Irrespective of their relationship with the deceased or the damages they seek, they are filled with every emotion imaginable: anger, frustration, sorrow, curiosity, and regret to name but a few. The death notification is sometimes the first knowledge the family has that the deceased was involved in criminal activity. Many times, the family lost touch with the person long ago or simply gave up trying to prevent the person from becoming involved in criminal activity. The stresses of alcohol abuse and drug addiction alone are enough to bring a family to its breaking point. When we add mental illness to the mix, many families are merely trying to hold on with impossible odds stacked against them.

In many cases, the lawsuit now becomes their personal mission. With the help of an attorney and the force of the courts, they can learn more about the life of a person they lost long before the LEO fired the first shot. Many times, the more they learn the more difficult the mission becomes and the harder it is for them to let go. At the same time, the litigants also learn more about law enforcement procedures than the public will ever know. Their lack of understanding "fuels the fire" that the death of their loved one was unnecessary or avoidable. Sometimes, they are unable to let go and dismiss their case even after the facts reveal that the LEO was legally justified in using deadly force. Remember that many times, the family will file suit even after the LEO has been cleared by an internal investigation, a criminal investigation, and a review of the use of force by the district attorney or the grand jury.

Important Terms for You to Know

When you started the academy, military service, or even the first grade, there were terms that were foreign to you. However, with time, you became familiar with the terminology of your new endeavor and environment. You also learned that the mastery of that terminology was essential to your success and avoidance of bad outcomes. The same is true about lawsuits. So, here we go. Dig in, keep an open mind, and do not get frustrated by the process. While it is a bit different from criminal procedure, it is pretty simple. There is another reason to learn about the civil process—no one is going to change the process for your lawsuit. New game? Time to learn the rules. Master the rules and you will master the game.

I will present these legal terms and concepts in the general order that they would occur or be employed during the process of a lawsuit.

Ante Litem Notice [pronounced like "Antie Light 'em"]

Written notice to a government entity that a person has a claim against that entity. The notice typically arrives via certified mail or overnight service. Although the requirements vary by state, the notice must outline the facts of the claim, the reason why the government entity is liable, the damages suffered by the person making the claim, and a demand for settlement within a specific time period. The notice must follow strict statutory guidelines or it is void. If a person fails to send an ante litem notice or fails to follow the proper procedure when sending the notice, the courts may prevent the person from filing some or all of their claims.

Cause of Action

A claim that a person has been injured or a request by a court to take some action. People commonly refer to a cause of action as a lawsuit. While people usually file a lawsuit seeking money damages based upon an injury, a person could also seek a writ of mandamus or an injunction. A writ of mandamus is an order from a court telling a person or an entity to do something, where an injunction is an order from a court telling a person or an entity not to do something.

A person sues for an injury like bruising, broken bones, or a violation of their rights, such as the constitutional right to be free from unlawful search and seizure. LEOs can be sued in federal or state courts and it really does not matter, in terms of severity, where the person files suit. Many times, these cases are brought in federal court pursuant to a federal statute that allows a person to sue for a violation of their constitutional rights. The statute, 42 U.S.C. § 1983, reads:

> Every person who, under color of any statute, ordinance, regulation, custom, or usage, of any State or Territory or the District of Columbia, subjects, or causes to be subjected, any citizen of the United States or other person within the jurisdiction thereof to the deprivation of any rights, privileges, or immunities secured by the Constitution and laws, shall be liable to the party injured in an action at law, suit in equity, or other proper proceeding for redress, except that in any action brought against a judicial officer for an act or omission taken in such officer's judicial capacity, injunctive relief shall not be granted unless a declaratory decree was

violated or declaratory relief was unavailable. For the purposes of this section, any Act of Congress applicable exclusively to the District of Columbia shall be considered to be a statute of the District of Columbia.

Remember that the LEO is not sued for violating 42 U.S.C. § 1983, as there is no penalty for violating this statute. This is a vehicle to address a "deprivation of any rights, privileges, or immunities secured by the Constitution and laws..." 42 U.S.C. § 1983. This is a technical distinction in the law, but you should be familiar with it as a professional LEO.

Plaintiff

The person who brings a cause of action. If the cause of action is a request for the court to take some action, like issue an injunction, the correct term is Petitioner.

Defendant

The person or entity against whom the cause of action is brought like the LEO, the agency, or the government entity. If the cause of action is a request for the court to take some action, like issue an injunction, the correct term is Respondent.

Summons

The document that commands a person or entity named in a lawsuit to formally answer or respond to the allegations contained in the lawsuit within a specified time. The summons usually states that if you do not formally answer the lawsuit and respond, the court may enter a judgment against you.

Complaint

The document that contains the formal allegations in the lawsuit. This document may be short or long. However, it is usually divided into paragraphs that set out the facts, as understood by the Plaintiff, and allegations against a LEO or an agency in the lawsuit.

Counterclaim

A claim filed against a person who files suit. For example, if you are involved in a fight with a suspect who later sues you for excessive use of force, you may be able to file a counterclaim against the suspect for the injuries you sustained in the fight.

Settlement and Discovery Conference

A mandatory meeting of the attorneys soon after the lawsuit is filed. During this meeting, the attorneys discuss the lawsuit, any potential for settlement, and a plan to learn more about the case from each other through a process known as discovery. This is a requirement in federal courts and in some state courts.

Initial Disclosures

Most common in federal court, initial disclosures are written statements filed soon after a lawsuit is filed. The disclosures list the names of the attorneys, the full, legal names of the parties, and other preliminary information.

Answer

The formal response to the allegations in the lawsuit. This document contains affirmative defenses to the lawsuit, as well as a response to each paragraph and allegation in the Complaint.

Affirmative Defenses

These are legal defenses to the lawsuit and are normally set out in the Answer. Many affirmative defenses are waived if not raised in the answer or by a formal motion filed with the Answer. There are several types of affirmative defenses based upon the nature of the defense. Some have the effect of forcing the person filing the lawsuit to go back and fix a defect and others, although rare, may allow a court to dismiss the lawsuit. There are several types of affirmative defenses:

Procedural Defense

A defense based upon the failure to follow proper procedure involved in filing, serving, or otherwise handling the lawsuit. For example, if a person failed to send an ante litem notice, this would be a procedural defense. If a person failed to properly serve you with a copy of the lawsuit or filed the lawsuit in the wrong court, your lawyer would raise a procedural defense. Another example is filing the lawsuit after the statute of limitations has expired.

Factual Defenses

Factual defenses are, as predicted, based upon the facts of the individual case. Lawyers are trained to ask this question, "What facts in the Complaint are inaccurate and what facts, if true, reduce or eliminate liability for my client?" For example, has the plaintiff sued the wrong Deputy Jones? Are the dates listed in the Complaint inaccurate? Has the Plaintiff sued the wrong governmental entity[56]? These are all defenses that can make a difference. While the Plaintiff can usually amend the Complaint to fix these factual issues, if they fail to do so, the case could be dismissed.

Immunity Defenses

Governments and government employees are entitled to immunity from lawsuits and damages in many instances. This immunity is based upon constitutional and statutory protection and reflects two overriding policies. First, governments perform functions that are critical to our society that no one else wants to perform. For example, few, if any, private companies would want to perform all duties of a sheriff's agency or fire agency. Second, society expects governments to perform certain functions and for that expectation, the law provides immunity for suits that would tie up government resources, including the government's money, which is really the people's money.

---

[56] I was involved in one case wherein a Plaintiff sued a building. To this day, I have no idea what the building allegedly did to him.

Entire textbooks exist on the topic of immunity afforded government employees, including LEOs. In order to provide you with the information you need without writing another textbook, I will provide a quick and simplified set of rules regarding immunity to give you a basic working knowledge of the concept.

Sometimes this immunity is expressed in a statute. For example, O.C.G.A. § 35-1-7 reads as follows:

> A law enforcement officer shall not be liable at law for any action or actions done while performing any duty at the scene of an emergency except for gross negligence, willful or wanton misconduct, or malfeasance. As used in this Code section, the term "law enforcement officer" means any peace officer who is employed by this state or any political subdivision thereof and who is required by the terms of his employment, whether by election or appointment, to give his full time to the preservation of public order or the protection of life and property or the prevention of crime. Such term shall include sheriffs and deputy sheriffs.

The law requires government actors to perform certain functions as a matter of course without much thought or discretion. When a function or task is required to be performed every time a situation arises in every instance, that task is said to be ministerial. A ministerial task is "An act performed without the independent exercise of discretion or judgment." If the act is mandatory, it is also termed a *ministerial duty*[57]. If an act requires some discretion on the part of the LEO, this is said to be a discretionary act. For example, the decision to prevent an intoxicated driver from leaving the scene of a traffic stop is a ministerial act. However, the decision to arrest the driver for DUI is a discretionary act.

The law generally provides no immunity for the failure to perform ministerial acts. However, the law generally does provide immunity for discretionary acts[58] unless the LEO acts recklessly or with the intent to injure another. In the law, no act requires more discretion than the decision to use force. So, in a use of force case, the Plaintiff will usually allege that you used excessive force such that your discretion should not protect you because you violated clearly established law[59]. Your defense, even if you violated a clearly established law, is that you acted with good faith in doing so. This principle was expressed in the central case on this issue, *Harlow v. Fitzgerald*, 457 U.S. 800 (1982) when the USSC stated, "government officials performing discretionary functions generally are shielded from liability for civil damages insofar as their conduct does not violate clearly established statutory or constitutional rights of which a reasonable person would have known[60]."

---

[57] Black's Law Dictionary 9th Ed. 2009.

[58] This is often called discretionary or qualified immunity. "A qualified immunity for a public official's acts, granted when the act in question required the exercise of judgment in carrying out official duties." Black's Law Dictionary 9th Ed. 2009.

[59] Qualified Immunity is "Immunity from civil liability for a public official who is performing a discretionary function, as long as the conduct does not violate clearly established constitutional or statutory rights." Black's Law Dictionary, 9th Ed. 2009.

[60] Id., 818.

A third type of immunity is usually called sovereign immunity. This is defined as "A government's immunity from being sued in its own courts without its consent[61]." Finally, there is a type of absolute or official immunity provided to certain officials by virtue of their office such as a judge for official acts or a prosecutor sued for an act taken in the course of prosecuting a case.

Discovery Period

This is the time during which the parties to the lawsuit exchange and gather information about the allegations and evidence of the other party. The amount of time varies based upon the court that has jurisdiction over the case and the facts of the case. The court can also extend the time for discovery. Generally, the initial discovery period is four months in federal court and six months in most state courts. The goal of discovery is to narrow the issues that will be presented at trial.

Interrogatories

Interrogatories are written questions exchanged by the parties to a lawsuit. Like any other discovery tool, interrogatories are intended to answer questions about the other party's case, obtain information that explains the other party's case, and obtain information that helps both parties assess the strength or weakness of their respective cases. Interrogatories can be very powerful. For example, a typical interrogatory in a use of force suit might be, "Please state the names of all persons who

---

[61] Black's Law Dictionary 9th Ed. 2009.

witnessed the events outlined in the Complaint." Someone from the party answering the interrogatories must swear under oath that the responses are true and correct to the best of his knowledge.

Requests for Production of Documents or "Things"

A list of documents or items, such as dispatch logs or 911 tapes, that the parties request in order to learn more about and assess the strength or weakness of the other party's case. For example, a typical request might be, "Please provide copies of the use of deadly force policy in place at your agency," or "Please provide a certified copy of the personnel files[62] of every employee who was on the scene of the shooting mentioned in the Complaint."

Requests for Admission

Requests for Admission ask the opposing party to admit or deny facts or verify that documents are authentic. For example, "Admit that Officer Jones was assigned to the Drug Interdiction Unit on the date of the shooting described in the Complaint." The parties are bound by their responses to Requests for Admission and they are perhaps the most powerful written discovery tool. Don't you wish you could use them with a suspect? As you can imagine, the lawsuit can move more quickly if the parties can obtain admissions about matters that help focus the remaining parts of the case.

---

[62] Attorneys can normally remove or "redact" social security numbers and dates of birth of spouses and children. Remind them to do so.

Deposition

A deposition is simply a question and answer session under oath. You will meet with your attorney to prepare you for the deposition. On the day of the deposition, you will appear at the office of your attorney or some other location and you will sit face to face across from the attorney for the Plaintiff. After the court reporter places you under oath, the attorney for the Plaintiff will ask you questions intending to learn more about you, your defenses, and how you intend to respond and defend the lawsuit. Perhaps the most important part of the deposition is the opportunity for the Plaintiff's attorney to see you and determine whether the jury will like you. Are you rude? Do you get angry when challenged? Are you dressed like a recruiting poster? Keep in mind that the plaintiff or his family are permitted to attend the deposition and the Plaintiff's attorney may arrange to record the deposition using a video camera. Just as the Plaintiff, you as the Defendant are also normally permitted to attend any deposition in the case if you are sued.

Expert

An expert is a person who has and can provide valuable, relevant information to the jury. The purpose is to assist the jury with matters that are "beyond the ken [knowledge] of the average juror[63]." The expert can possess this information

---

[63] Federal Rule of Evidence 702.

based upon knowledge, training, skill, or experience[64]. For example, in a use of force case, an expert may be a firearms instructor, a medical examiner, or a scientist trained in ballistics. Simply put, you cannot expect the average juror to understand how it is possible to determine where a person was standing at the time they fired a semiautomatic firearm based solely upon the location of the fired brass. An expert can explain this concept to the jury, and the jury can then use that knowledge to arrive at their decision.

The role of the expert is to explain information and educate the jury or the judge to assist them in their decision. They typically perform this task by reviewing all materials relevant to the case. In many cases, the expert is permitted to review and rely upon evidence that is not admissible at trial for the purpose of forming her opinion[65]. As you may have guessed, both sides will use experts to educate the jury. However, an expert must refrain from becoming an advocate for any party.

Expert witnesses come from every source imaginable on nearly every topic that can be covered during a trial. Some are college professors, some are scientists, and some are retired LEOs. Some hold professional licenses and others rely on their experience in an area.

Prior to the trial of the case, the expert will form opinions that are relevant to the case. Each side is required, if asked or as a matter of course in federal courts, to disclose the opinions and anticipated

---

[64] Federal Rule of Evidence 702.
[65] Id., 703.

testimony of their expert. Prior to trial, the expert will typically sit for a deposition so that the opposing side can explore those opinions, challenge those opinions, and evaluate the strength of their case in light of those opinions. This can be a pivotal point in any case. Many lawsuits settle or are dismissed following the depositions of the experts. Those depositions are also heavily relied upon during the summary judgment phase, which I will explain below.

You may and should be asked to look at the opinions and reports of the expert retained by your attorney and the opposing experts, as well. As a LEO, you possess knowledge, training, skill, and experience beyond that of the average juror. Your attorneys should welcome your input and you should help them.

As an example, I once assisted an attorney representing a LEO who was sued for shooting a juvenile. The juvenile stabbed the LEO, so it was a good shoot. Both the LEO and the suspect were lucky to be alive. The attorney representing the LEO had never seen any of the training materials regarding edged weapons, the speed with which a suspect with an edged weapon can deploy the weapon, or a true demonstration of why an edged weapon is a lethal threat at a distance of twenty-one feet away from the LEO. We provided the attorney with a few videos and he got the message loud and clear. You must take an active role in your case and help your attorney defeat and challenge the opposing expert while bolstering your expert's testimony at trial.

Motion for Summary Judgment

A motion is a request for a court to take some action. A Motion for Summary Judgment usually is one of the first filed by the Defendant and asks a court to dispose of a lawsuit, or part of the lawsuit, by examining the facts that are not in dispute and applying the law to those facts. If there is a dispute about the facts, the court is not permitted to grant the Motion for Summary Judgment because the jury must decide the facts of the case based upon the testimony and evidence presented to them. Many use of force cases are dismissed after the attorney for the LEO and the agency files a Motion for Summary Judgment asking the court to find that the LEO and the agency are entitled to immunity from suit.

Damages

Damages is a general term used to describe money sought through a lawsuit. This can consist of attorney fees, expenses of litigation, and money awarded to the plaintiff. Damages are divided into three classes, special, general, and punitive. Expenses of litigation and attorney fees are a special type of damages.

Special Damages

These are damages that can be documented with a receipt or that can be drawn out on a blackboard. For example, medical bills the Plaintiff incurred can be shown to the jury and the total can be drawn on a blackboard. Other examples are lost wages, funeral expenses, and medical equipment, such as a wheelchair.

General damages

General damages sought by the Plaintiff are those that cannot be reduced to a number and for which there is no receipt are known as general damages. The most common example is pain and suffering. The measure of general damages is determined by "the enlightened conscience of a fair and impartial jury[66]." The jury can award an amount of money for pain and suffering, even if that number is unrelated to the special damages.

Punitive damages

Punitive damages are special class of damages intended to punish behavior that is intentional, wanton, or reckless[67].

Loss of Consortium

The legal spouse of a Plaintiff is entitled to recover for the loss of services of that spouse. For example, if a spouse is required to take over duties that the Plaintiff normally would have done, like cooking, cleaning, or yard work, the jury can award money damages to the spouse.

---

[66] O.C.G.A. 51-12-12; 13 Ga. Jur. Personal Injury and Torts § 11:14

[67] Punitive damages may be awarded only in such tort actions in which it is proven by clear and convincing evidence that the defendant's actions showed willful misconduct, malice, fraud, wantonness, oppression, or that entire want of care which would raise the presumption of conscious indifference to consequences...Punitive damages shall be awarded not as compensation to a plaintiff but solely to punish, penalize, or deter a defendant. O.C.G.A. § 51-12-5.1.

Mediation

Typically, this is a non-binding process through which a third party, also known as a neutral, gathers the parties together and attempts to reach a settlement. Non-binding means that the neutral does not decide the outcome, but works to hopefully find a resolution agreeable to both parties. While some courts order the parties to participate in mediation, many times the parties agree to do so voluntarily. Mediation can take place at any phase of the lawsuit. However, it is commonly scheduled after discovery is completed and just before trial.

Jury Trial vs. Bench Trial

In most trials, the jury determines the facts that will be applied to reach a verdict and then returns a verdict. The judge determines what evidence can be considered and what law the jury will apply to reach their decision. In some cases, the parties can agree to allow the judge to perform both functions and the case will go forward without a jury. When there is no jury, the case is known as a bench trial.

Jury Selection or Voir Dire

This is the process of asking questions, through a survey or in person, of a group of potential jurors to select a group that will be fair and impartial in their decisions. Pronunciation of "Voir Dire" varies greatly across the United States.

Jury Charges

When the case involves a jury, the judge will decide what law the jury will use to reach their decision. While the jury is not in the courtroom, the parties present principles of law to the judge near the end of the trial based upon the issues in the case and the evidence presented during the trial. The judge selects what law she will present to the jury when the case is over, right before they retire to the jury room to deliberate. The judge will also present general principles of law that apply to every trial, such as the effect of witness testimony, the role of experts, and how to resolve conflicts in the evidence.

Verdict

The verdict is the decision of the jury or of the judge if there is no jury in the case.

Appeal

An appeal is the procedure utilized to challenge the decision of a court. Generally, this involves asking a higher court to change or reverse the decision of the lower court. The courts that make the initial decision in a case, with or without a jury, are known as trial courts. The higher courts are known as appellate courts. The highest appellate court in the United States is the United States Supreme Court.

The Attorney for the LEO...and the Agency

Suits against LEOs are handled by a variety of lawyers. Some are employees of the government entity, while others are hired by the government entity to handle that particular case. A third type of attorney is hired by the insurance company that the government agency pays to defend the agency in these types of cases. This insurance is like car, homeowners, or other types of insurance. Governments buy an insurance policy to protect the assets of the government that belong to the citizens and to ensure that lawyers are assigned to defend the lawsuit. As with your car insurance, the insurance company provides lawyers to defend the claims and appear in court on behalf of the government entity. In most cases, these attorneys will also defend you in a suit.

The question always comes up in any class I teach, "Do I need my own insurance policy?" The short answer is, "It depends." It is important to remember that your insurance company performs two valuable functions. The company provides an attorney to defend you. The company will also pay a judgment or settlement on your behalf up to the limits of the policy. This is called indemnification. For example, if you are 100 percent at fault in a car wreck, your car insurance company will provide an attorney to defend any lawsuit that arises from that wreck. The company will also likely pay any settlement or judgment from a jury that stems from that lawsuit. However, this payment is limited by the amount of insurance coverage you have. If a jury returns a verdict against you for $1,000,000 and your car insurance has a limit of $100,000, in most cases, you are responsible for the remaining $900,000.

You can obtain an attorney to defend you through a legal defense plan, as well. These plans provide a lawyer to defend you in a civil suit, but they do not pay any settlements or judgments against you. So, as outlined in the example above, the legal defense plan will pay for a lawyer to defend you, but it will not indemnify you. There are several legal defense plans offered. You should choose one carefully based upon its affiliation with law enforcement cases, the financial stability of the plan, your ability to choose your own attorney, the limits of the plan, and the ability for you to contact the plan administrators directly if there is a problem. The Fraternal Order of Police has an excellent Legal Defense Program. You can find more information on the web at foplegal.com. The Fraternal Order of Police Legal Defense Plan is run by the Fraternal Order of Police.

In general, the attorneys who defend these cases are highly experienced. In many states, the attorneys who defend one agency may sue agencies in other parts of the state. I'll leave that discussion for another time. However, especially when the attorneys are brought to the table by an insurance company, the counsel handling your case will be very familiar with the law, your defenses, and the civil process.

Nearly every attorney who handles these cases will rely upon a hired expert to defend you. This expert will educate and guide the attorney as she learns about the case, answers the lawsuit, and prepares for trial. It is nearly impossible to handle a use of force case without an expert on behalf of the LEO or the agency, so employing an expert does not mean the attorney is inexperienced or cannot handle the case. She is not able to represent you in the trial and also provide expert testimony. So at trial, this expert will explain terms, concepts, and strategies to the jury to assist them as they decide the case.

While we are on the topic, under no circumstances should you represent or defend yourself in a suit following an OIS. The legal procedure alone is far too complicated to learn as you go. Even if you have been involved in a dozen suits, the law changes and each case is very fact-specific. Defending yourself is like buying a "Neurosurgery at Home Kit." You might save money, but the outcome will not be pleasant. One last point to drive the concept home: If I were facing a suit following an OIS, I would hire an attorney to represent me.

The Attorney for the Plaintiffs

The varied reasons for filing lawsuits should tell you something: most people will not dismiss their lawsuits voluntarily. You should not expect them to go away without a fight. They usually believe they are right, and the law requires that they sign their lawsuit to attest to their good faith belief in the allegations. However, as I stated above, they can be wrong for a bunch of reasons. Sometimes, lawsuits are filed because of misunderstandings.

Not once in law school did we discuss the concept of a use of force continuum, the effect of lighting upon a LEO's ability to perceive and respond to a threat, or proper law enforcement procedures following the use of deadly force by a LEO. Do *not* expect that an attorney who files a lawsuit against you or your agency will understand these concepts. The lawyers hire experts to educate them about law enforcement standards and procedures. While most experts are competent, professional, and trustworthy, some are not and only tell the lawyer what the lawyer wants to hear. As you can imagine, this is problematic. Here is an example from an actual case I handled.

An attorney for the family of a suspect shot and killed by a LEO filed a civil suit against the LEO and the agency. He also had his client take steps to seek a criminal warrant for the LEO for the death of the suspect. In Georgia, whenever a private citizen seeks to take a warrant for someone, the court must hold a hearing known as a "pre-arrest hearing." This is essentially a probable cause hearing. The judge decides if the matter is criminal in nature or should be handled by the civil courts. The judge also decides if there is probable cause to believe that a crime occurred and if the person against whom the warrant is sought committed that crime. See O.C.G.A. § 17-7-20. In this case, the pre-arrest hearing took place before a superior court judge[68]. During the course of the six and a half hour hearing[69], the attorney for the family questioned the Georgia Bureau of Investigation agent who investigated the shooting as to the lack of warning the LEO gave prior to firing.

Imagine my surprise when the attorney for the family asked the following question:

> *[Isn't it] standard procedure for an officer before he fires a gun to just give a warning to tell people, get your hands up, I'm going to shoot you[70]?*

---

[68] Georgia law requires that a probate judge, state court judge, or superior court judge hear any request for the arrest of a LEO in the performance of official duties. O.C.G.A. § 17-4-40(c).

[69] The LEO was cleared of any criminal wrongdoing. The judge found the use of force was reasonable and the shooting death justifiable. The suspect was unarmed.

[70] In Re: Jeffrey Deal, Superior Court of Laurens County September 8, 2011, Transcript P. 127 Lines 9-11.

I was amazed at the question, as was the Georgia Bureau of Investigation agent and the district attorney. The lawyer for the family had been practicing law for more than twenty years. He was either misinformed or uninformed. However, if he and his client truly believed that the law required such a warning, you can understand why he came to court that day. Lesson learned.

What types of attorneys file suits against LEOs and agencies? Well, all types. Some handle all types of claims on behalf of people who are injured, while some handle only cases against LEOs. Some believe that LEOs should not be allowed to use deadly force at all, and some are former LEOs. They take these cases for a variety of reasons. If they win, they receive a contingency fee, meaning they are paid a percentage of the settlement or verdict plus the reimbursement of their expenses. Those expenses can be significant. It can cost $100,000 or more to bring a case to trial against a LEO or agency. In some cases, if they receive a verdict of one dollar, they will still be paid their fees and expenses based upon an hourly rate. The system is intended to allow poor people to bring suits to address a violation of their rights. The same is true of most lawsuits for discrimination in the workplace and in many contract disputes. This is why some agencies settle even when they believe the case is defendable or the damages are very low.

What Should You Expect from the Attorney Representing You in a Lawsuit

"A lawyer shall not represent or continue to represent a client if there is a significant risk that the...lawyer's duties to another client...will materially and adversely affect the representation of the client." "Loyalty is an essential element in the lawyer's relationship to a client." So begins Rule 1.7 of the Georgia Rules of Professional Conduct and Comment 1 to same rule. These rules govern the conduct of attorneys as they represent clients. Simply stated, a lawyer must provide independent representation to each client.

I receive a lot of calls from LEOs who are concerned that the lawyer representing them is also representing the agency. They wonder whether the lawyer hired by or selected for the agency by an insurance company, or the county or city attorney, can represent two clients: the LEO and the agency. This is especially true when the LEO determines that she is not paying the lawyer's fee. While this is a normal concern, there is generally little to worry about.

Lawyers routinely represent multiple clients, companies, and employees at the same time. The loyalty owed to anyone represented is not affected by who is paying the fees and expenses of litigation. The lawyer owes an independent duty to the client[71]. Unless the interests of the clients diverge or begin to compete against each other, the attorney is able to represent the agency and the LEO or LEOs who are sued. However, if the interests of the clients diverge, then the LEO may need a separate attorney. For example, if the LEO violated policy or a law, it may be difficult for one attorney to represent the LEO and the agency. If you are assigned a separate attorney, the agency or the insurance company should continue to pay for the attorney and the expenses of litigation. It is very rare for a

---

[71] Georgia Rules of Professional Conduct 2.1. The Georgia Rules of Professional Conduct are modeled after those promulgated by the American Bar Association. These rules are generally standard throughout the United States.

LEO to be forced to defend himself when the agency is also sued. This is the case even after you have left the agency.

There are three things you should expect from the lawyer representing you: access, communication, and advice. You should have access to the attorney when you have questions, when events occur that require action on your part, and whenever you feel like you need access. You should *never* be required to go through your chain of command to contact the attorney representing you in a civil suit.

Communication with the attorney is required. You should be informed about the status of the case, the good and bad points of the case, and the events coming in the future. You should also be clear about the strategy for handling the lawsuit. Finally, lawyers, although they are known in our society by many names, give advice. As this is a book for LEOs, I will allow you to pause now for a chuckle and an opportunity to think of several words you have used in the past to describe lawyers[72].

Now that you are back with us, lawyers are known as attorneys and counselors. The word attorney comes from the fact that lawyers are agents of a client and act on behalf the client. A lawyer is one who represents clients in legal matters and provides advice. Counselor is also an appropriate term to describe the role of a lawyer. At the essence of your relationship with a lawyer, you should receive advice. What can I expect from this process? What are the risks and benefits of the strategies and available options? How long will this lawsuit take? What will happen at the end of the lawsuit? These and many others are all reasonable questions for you to ask and have

---

[72] Best quote in this regard: "I hate lawyers, but I love *MY* lawyer!"

answered irrespective of who is paying the lawyer's bill. Remember, a client is defined as "one that is under the protection of another[73]." If you ever feel that the lawyer is not meeting the three requirements outlined in this paragraph, say something.

You also have an obligation to be accessible to your attorney. Provide your cell, home, and work numbers along with your email addresses. Make certain your lawyer is aware of any vacation, training, or other situations that will limit your accessibility. Finally, if you have more than one lawyer, make certain they are able to contact each other.

The last item I want to bring up is time spent with the lawyer at critical milestones in the case. For example, you should have an in-depth discussion with the attorney prior to the filing of the answer, prior to your deposition, prior to mediation, and prior to trial. By in-depth, I mean in-person, uninterrupted, and ending only when your questions have been answered and you feel fully informed and prepared. Remember that preparation is a two-way street. You should know the relevant policies and reports better than anyone.

Knowing why someone decided to sue you will not make it easier to be served, hire an attorney, or litigate the case, but it may help you prevent the suit before they file. Write clear and detailed reports, take the extra steps to preserve video and other evidence of your actions, and do not hesitate to meet with people who want answers after an event. In my experience, the people who are looking for answers make the toughest plaintiffs because the truth may be more upsetting than they expected.

---

[73] http://www.merriam-webster.com/dictionary/client

Service of a Lawsuit

I will admit that some of the most fun I had working as an Investigator with the Cobb County Solicitor General's Office was spent serving subpoenas. I also enjoyed arresting people for practicing law without a license while I was attending law school at night. While most of the time the process was straightforward, my favorite cases involved the folks who wanted to avoid being served. I posed as a disgruntled customer, a neighbor, and a careless driver who hit a car in the parking lot. Bottom line: Anyone can be served.

When it comes to lawsuits, service of process is extremely important. Although you may be accustomed to receiving subpoenas through interoffice mail or some other informal method, being served with a lawsuit is serious business. Our legal system has strict rules about the service of lawsuits because the court generally does not have any authority over you in a civil case until you are properly served. This is a concept called personal jurisdiction. There are complicated rules about who can serve lawsuits, where the suit must be filed, and what court can hear the suit. In short, the person filing suit must properly navigate the rules or his lawsuit may be dismissed. Once you are served with the lawsuit, you have your own set of obligations with serious consequences if you fail to act properly.

When you are served, the clock starts ticking! You generally have thirty days in a state court, or twenty days in federal court, to file an answer to the allegations in the lawsuit. That answer must also contain, in most instances, all legal defenses to the lawsuit. This is a short period of time in which you must gather important documents, verify the allegations in the lawsuit, and decide what legal defenses you may raise.

By now, you realize that you should contact a lawyer when you are served with a lawsuit. Here are my tips regarding service of process:

1. Never authorize anyone to accept service of a lawsuit on your behalf without speaking with an attorney.

2. If you are served, immediately take everything you are given when you are served and place it into an envelope.

3. Immediately write down the following on the envelope: the date and time and a description of the person who served you.

4. Get your calendar and make three notes: the day you were served, twenty days from the date upon which you were served and thirty days from the date upon which you were served. Write those three dates on the envelope.

5. Bring all of the documents you received to your chain of command AND your own attorney. If you are a member of the Fraternal Order of Police, contact your lodge president for an appointment with the lodge attorney. If you are a member of the Fraternal Order of Police Legal Defense Plan or you have your own professional liability insurance, notify the plan representative or your insurance company *exactly* as

required by the insurance policy or the contract.

6. Make certain that you have all of the relevant documents and evidence, such as incident reports, indictments, and video recordings available for the attorney.

7. Do not sign ANYTHING without checking with an attorney.

8. Follow up with the attorney to make certain that an answer was timely filed on your behalf. The attorney should not be at all upset with your efforts to stay on top of the case.

9. Do not discuss the details of the lawsuit with anyone except your attorney or your chain of command as ordered to do so, and do not provide recorded statements, by phone or in person, without an attorney present.

10. Direct all media inquires to the agency's chain of command or public information officer. This can be challenging. I have represented LEOs who were confronted by the media at their homes following the filing of a lawsuit. Be polite, be professional, assume you are being recorded and say nothing.

The LEO as a Plaintiff – Filing a Counterclaim

You also have a limited amount of time to decide whether you can, or want to, file a counterclaim. A counterclaim is a claim filed against a party who files suit against you. In most instances, you must file the counterclaim with your answer. I am a big fan of counterclaims against people who sue LEOs. However, if you wait too long, the court may reject your counterclaim.

The LEO as a Plaintiff – Filing a Claim

While counterclaims can be an effective tool, you should know that LEOs are not required to wait until they are sued to seek damages against a perpetrator when they are injured in the line of duty. I have had the honor to represent many LEOs in many types of cases. I've stood with LEOs in grand juries, trial courts, civil service boards, and internal affairs interviews. I have also stood and protected LEOs and their families when they were injured on the job. I'm not just talking about workers compensation cases. I'm talking about using the civil courts to recover money damages for LEOs injured on the job.

Most of these cases involve motor vehicle collisions. In these cases, you would have a potential civil suit against the driver who ran the red light or caused the wreck. You may also have a claim against the driver's employer. These claims often settle without the need for a civil suit, especially when people pull out in front of LEOs. It is hard to say you did not see the marked car coming. Juries are very unforgiving of people who injure LEOs, especially DUI drivers. In fact, I have recovered six and seven figure settlements for LEOs injured by DUI drivers.

However, not all LEOs I represent are injured in car wrecks. I sued on behalf of a LEO in response to a use of force claim filed by a young man and his parents after the LEO shot the young man. The LEO shot several times after the young man stabbed him. I sued the perpetrator for the stabbing and the parents for buying the knife. I also sued a person who falsely alleged that a LEO fondled her on a traffic stop. We were successful in both cases and many others.

Civil suits are nearly always available to LEOs whenever they are injured by the actions of another. Sometimes, the suits do not make monetary sense, but often this is the only way for the LEO to clear his name. In the case of the LEO falsely accused of fondling a woman on a traffic stop, he now has a copy of the civil judgment against his accuser in his personnel file. No lingering questions hanging over his head or rumors during promotion reviews. He was cleared. His accuser also has to write him a check every month.

Civil suits are separate and apart from a claim under workers compensation. Workers compensation is a no-fault system. If you are working and suffer an injury, the workers compensation system is there to ensure that your medical bills and other benefits are paid. However, you can file a claim for workers compensation *and* a civil suit against the person who injured you. In most states, however, you cannot sue *your* employer in a separate civil suit.

The important thing is to find an attorney who is not working for your agency or government entity. You must find an attorney who will independently evaluate the merits of your case. In my experience, agencies do not mind if you file suit against a person who injures you and are generally very supportive. This is especially the case when you file a countersuit against a person who sues you for excessive use of force. Remember that the suspect who punches and kicks you can be sued. That is the basis of your countersuit when that same suspect sues you for excessive use of force after you arrest him. The filing of a countersuit changes the dynamics of the lawsuit.

Finally, the attorney you choose must be willing to go the extra mile. I once represented a LEO who was shot serving a warrant. He and his partner were able to exit the house. The suspect took his own life after the responding LEOs formed a perimeter. I wanted to file suit against the suspect's estate, but the family tried to prevent this by refusing to set up an estate. So, I set up an estate for the suspect, appointed an attorney to represent the estate, and filed suit against the suspect's estate! It took more than two years, but we were able to collect a settlement for the LEO. He is still working today, and I am proud to know that I helped him.

I learned many things in law school and I learned a lot on the street as a LEO. I practice law with a philosophy I lived by on the street: "Never give up." Do not forget to consider a civil suit if you are injured on duty. This is so important to protect yourself and your family, as you may not be able to work part-time jobs or earn any overtime while out of work. A recovery in a civil suit can help fill those gaps, especially if you are not able to return to work. Read my blog post on uninsured/ underinsured motorist (UM) insurance to make certain you are doing everything possible to protect yourself as your personal car insurance may be available to help you if you are injured in a car wreck on duty. You are a part of our court system, civil and criminal. Do not hesitate to use that system to help you if you are injured on or off duty. You deserve access to our courts. In fact, you earn that access every day.

I'll See You in Court!

If you have been a LEO for more than five minutes, someone has probably threatened to sue you. While the context changes from domestic disputes to the execution of search warrants and complicated arrests, LEOs hear the threats of litigation all too often. I receive about one call per month from a LEO who is concerned that someone may sue. So, how do you separate the people who will sue from the people who only threaten to sue? What can you do to protect yourself when you believe the threat is credible?

Receiving a threat from a suspect about a lawsuit is like hearing that a person soon to obtain the title of "arrestee" is a black belt. Although you hear it all the time, you should proceed with caution. Although many people theorize that only rich people sue, this is not reality. In the real word, lawsuits are filed against LEOs by people of all means and socioeconomic standing. Folks with the means to sue are likely to do so. However, many groups exist to assist *anyone*, regardless of their means, who wants to sue a LEO. Many suits against LEOs are also filed by inmates. The short answer is there is no way to be certain whether someone will carry through on a threat to sue.

With any threat, of litigation or otherwise, take precautions. You should realize that it is relatively easy for anyone to file a lawsuit against a LEO. So, check state and federal court records online to find out if the one threatening to sue you has filed suit in the past. In addition, make certain that your official report is thorough and take some time to preserve the evidence that will protect you. Make certain that you have a copy of the dashboard video, audiotape of telephone calls, or any other evidence that you fear may be misplaced or be destroyed over time in the normal course of business. Keep track of the criminal case as it moves through the legal process and keep an open line of communication with the prosecutor. Make certain that the prosecutor knows that this defendant threatened to file suit. Finally, you should also get a certified[74] copy of the prosecutor's file when the criminal case is complete and keep it for your records. You should do the same for any related files regarding any internal investigations that involve the defendant who threatened to sue.

Finally, look out for letters from the individual's attorney or requests issued to your agency demanding certified copies of documents, especially your internal affairs or personnel file. Notify your chain of command if you receive any letters or notices regarding the case. This is essential to make certain that your agency can properly defend you. You should also speak with a private attorney to make certain that your interests are properly protected. If you are a member of the Fraternal Order of Police, you should notify your lodge executive board and the representative of your legal defense plan.

The most important thing to remember is that being sued is not fair, but life's not fair. The fire department gets to a house, chops holes in the roof, and the homeowner brings a cake to the fire station the next day. LEOs may save a life and be sued anyway. A cop's life isn't so glamorous, but we knew this when we signed up for the job.

---

[74] A certified copy of a document contains a sworn statement prepared by a person in charge of keeping the documents that demonstrates the document is a true and correct copy of the official document.

Lance LoRusso

Filing the Answer

The formal response to a lawsuit is called the Answer. Now I know what you are thinking, but this is a legal response to the allegations in the lawsuit. Although you may prefer to provide a response similar to the famous defense opening in My Cousin Vinny, "Everything that guy just said is bullshit," such a response would not be productive! You can give that response, but use your "inside my head" voice.

The formal response to a lawsuit is important. The biggest complaint I hear from LEOs is that the lawyer for their agency was not aggressive enough when responding to the lawsuit. Answering a lawsuit takes a great deal of time, strategy, and finesse. Most courts also require you to assert defenses called affirmative defenses, some of which are lost if you do not assert them in your Answer. In short, filing an Answer to a lawsuit is probably best left to the lawyers. However, your input is important.

At a minimum, you should meet with the attorney filing the Answer on your behalf. Why? Simply put, because you were there and the lawyer was not. The allegations in the lawsuit will be based upon a set of facts. These facts are usually set out in the lawsuit. These facts may be inaccurate for a number of reasons. The Answer is your first opportunity to correct those inaccuracies or, at the very least, put the opposing lawyer on notice that the facts will be in dispute. This will be important later in the lawsuit.

You should also meet with the lawyer to ensure that she is aware of all of the evidence available for your defense. Do not assume that the attorney hired by your agency or by you personally is aware of all of the evidence that you can use for your defense. For example, do not assume that

142

the lawyer is aware of the information available from a TASER download or the tremendous support available from TASER International. A great litigator may have no experience with firearms or pursuit driving. I routinely field calls personally or as General Counsel for the Georgia Fraternal Order of Police from attorneys who seek "hands-on information" they can use to defend LEOs. Share the evidence you preserved, and any other evidence you know exists, to help with your defense.

Finally, do not be afraid to ask questions. Does the lawyer believe you did anything wrong? Does she believe this lawsuit is frivolous? Has this person filed other suits against LEOs? Do you need your own attorney as I discussed above?

The Answer is the first step in your defense. Get involved, stay involved, and be prepared to go the distance.

Lawsuit v. Reality

When I was on patrol, I was always amused when the news reported on an incident that I responded to or handled. Many times, I remember telling my wife that the report had little to do with what happened on the scene. However, I must admit those news reports were often more interesting. Such is often the case when you first read a lawsuit filed against you.

When you read the lawsuit, you will hear some legal language at the beginning. This language usually relates to jurisdiction of the court. Next, you will find a set of paragraphs that set out the facts of the lawsuit. Like those news stories I referenced earlier, you may disagree with the facts. Disagree may be a strange choice of word. The facts set out in the lawsuit may, in fact, set you off! I have pulled LEOs off the ceiling when they read the facts set out in a lawsuit. My goal in this section is to, well, keep you away from your ceiling fan.

There are a few reasons why the facts set out in a lawsuit are not the same facts you recall or those set out in your incident report. First, the lawyers get the facts from their client the plaintiff. Need I say more? Yes, I am saying that the guy you arrested at a .24 BAC[75] is entitled to file a lawsuit based upon *his* recollection of what happened. Second, the client tells his lawyer what he remembers. Anyone who has worked a car wreck knows that every version of the facts will be slightly different. In fact, Georgia juries are told that they must make every effort to reconcile different versions of events by witnesses without assuming a witness is lying[76]. Yet another reason the facts in the lawsuit are far from what you remember is that your incident report may not properly document the events. Enough said.

The rest of the lawsuit contains the legal reasons for the suit, such as allegations of excessive force or wrongful death, and a prayer for relief. The prayer can include a request for money and attorney fees. Some lawsuits vary, but essentially these parts set out what the plaintiff says you did wrong and why he should win in court. This is part of the lawyer's role as an advocate. Any fact can be stated in a persuasive manner to best fit the case.

The lesson to learn here is that you must remain calm. I recently worked with a LEO defending a suit in which the plaintiff left out a critical point in his "facts." That critical

---

[75] Blood alcohol content.

[76] If you do find conflicts in the evidence, it would be your duty under the law to reconcile these conflicts if possible. You should reconcile these conflicts without attributing perjury or false statements to anyone. You should reconcile these conflicts, if you can, as if each witness had spoken the truth. Conflicts in Evidence, Georgia Suggested Pattern Jury Instructions –Civil 00.060

point was the reason for the traffic stop. That's a pretty important fact if I was paying attention in the academy and law school. Whether you are accused of arresting a person without probable cause, excessive force, or driving the getaway Bronco for OJ, don't let it get to you. Get a legal team together, prepare to defend the lawsuit and keep your eye on the important things in life, like coming home at the end of your shift.

When a LEO is sued, he is usually defended by the city attorney, the county attorney, the attorney general's office, or by a law firm selected by his agency to handle the case. Those lawyers represent two clients—the government that you work for and you. As stated earlier, as long as your interests do not conflict with your employer's interests, the same lawyer can represent both you and your employer. However, when a conflict arises, you must have your own independent attorney.

Do not expect the attorney provided by your agency to represent you before a grand jury looking into your use of force, or during a criminal inquiry by the federal government for a civil rights complaint. The attorney representing your agency simply cannot offer independent advice to you in these situations because the outcome could adversely affect your agency.

Sometimes, the conflict of interest is more subtle. What if three officers faced an armed subject at similar distances and only one used deadly force? While this may not indicate that the one officer acted improperly, it could create a conflict that requires that officer to have his own attorney.

Here is the takeaway for Leos:

1. Do not expect the lawyer provided by your agency to represent you in any criminal inquiry or during an internal investigation.

2. Ask the attorney appointed to represent you if she believes there is a potential for a conflict of interest now or later in the case.

3. Consult your own attorney early in the process to get independent advice about conflicts of interest and to allow him to step in should a conflict arise later.

Courts Pay Attention to the Facts and the Reality of Life on the Street

In 2007, the USSC released a decision in the case of *Scott v. Harris*, 550 U.S. 372 (2007). The case is critical in the analysis of use of force and immunity afforded to LEOs sued for excessive use of force[77]. Perhaps most important is the fact that the USSC discussed in detail the role and importance of video footage from the LEO's in-car camera in the analysis of excessive force claims and efforts by the LEO to dismiss[78] the claims based upon qualified immunity. The Court examined the question of whether a LEO who used force to end a pursuit was entitled to

[77] The case also has important implications for LEOs seeking dismissal of cases filed against them at the summary judgment phase.

[78] These motions are typically filed as Motions for Summary Judgment. This is a motion filed in federal or state courts that seeks an order from the court by asking the judge to look at the law, examine the facts, and make a decision. Often the lawyer for the LEO asks the court to dismiss the case entirely. The court is not permitted to grant summary judgment on any issue as to which there is a "genuine issue of material fact" because factual disputes are resolved by juries, rather than judges. F.R.C.P. 56.

qualified immunity. At the end, the Court not only found the LEO was entitled to qualified immunity and dismissed the case, but the Court also ordered that the in-car video be made part of the official record for the first time in history. The Court also held that courts were entitled, if not encouraged, to look at the in-car video as an objective view of what occurred. In short, the Court refused to allow the person suing the LEO to put forth a version of the facts that contradicted the in-car video in an attempt to survive a motion for summary judgment.

In *Harris*, a Coweta County Sheriff's Deputy intentionally struck a suspect's vehicle during a chase with the intent to end the chase. The chase ended, but the suspect was seriously injured. The suspect sued the deputy and his agency seeking money damages alleging that the deputy used excessive force. The perpetrator's attorneys argued before the Court that the deputy's use of force was unreasonable in part because it was not authorized by the *Tennessee v. Garner*[79] decision. In short, the perpetrator's attorneys argued that a speeding vehicle is not the same as an armed, fleeing felon and the LEO was not justified in using his vehicle to intentionally end the chase.

The USSC rejected this argument stating, "*Garner* did not establish a magical on/off switch that triggers rigid preconditions whenever an officer's actions constitute "deadly force." *Garner* was simply an application of the Fourth Amendment's "reasonableness" test..." In arriving at this decision, the USSC used a relative culpability test and asked the following questions: What actions did the perpetrator take? What actions did the LEO take? What actions did the bystanders take? Who created the risk of

---

[79] 471 U.S. 1(1985)

injury? Who was placed at risk? The language of the decision, written by Justice Scalia states,

"It was [the perpetrator], after all, who intentionally placed himself and the public in danger by unlawfully engaging in the reckless, high-speed flight that ultimately produced the choice between two evils that Scott confronted.

...

"Multiple police cars, with blue lights flashing and sirens blaring, had been chasing [the perpetrator] for nearly 10 miles, but he ignored their warning to stop. By contrast, those who might have been harmed had Scott not taken the action he did were entirely innocent. We have little difficulty in concluding it was reasonable for Scott to take the action that he did.

...

"The car chase that [the perpetrator] initiated in this case posed a substantial and immediate risk of serious physical injury to others; no reasonable jury could conclude otherwise. Scott's attempt to terminate the chase by forcing [the perpetrator] off the road was reasonable, and Scott is entitled to [be dismissed from the lawsuit].

There are several important points in the *Harris* decision. First, as set out above, the USSC says that courts are encouraged to look to the objective version of events available from the LEO's in-car camera when determining if there is a genuine dispute about the facts of the case. Second, the Court again stated that LEOs will not be judged by a rigid set of rules regarding the use of force, as LEOs operate in rapidly changing environments and must constantly assess and reassess their actions in light of the Fourth Amendment's reasonableness standard. Trainers will be familiar with this concept as outlined in the case of *Graham v. Conner*[80]. Third, the USSC stated that the actions of the perpetrator in a chase should be the subject of judicial review, and the court should consider whether the LEO's actions were reasonable in terminating the chase based upon the relative risk posed by the perpetrator to the public and the LEO. Fourth, the Court refused to restrict *Tennessee v. Garner* to fleeing, armed felons, and instead held that *Garner* stands for the proposition that the use of force by LEOs will be judged at all times by the reasonableness of that force and not according to a strict set of rules and guidelines. Finally, the USSC court proved, once again, that the Court will take the time to examine the realities of law enforcement, respect the job and decisions made by LEOs every day, and will afford the profession due deference when a LEO acts in a reasonable and professional manner and articulates the reasons for his actions.

Immunity Afforded by Statute

Sometimes, a legislature will make specific efforts to provide immunity to LEOs thorough a statute. While the state constitution is also a statute that affords immunity, we will explore a specific effort in Georgia to provide

---

[80] 490 U.S. 386 (1989).

immunity to LEOs. In keeping with the subject matter in *Scott v. Harris*, we will explore immunity set out in a Georgia law related to vehicle pursuits and the use of emergency vehicles. Your state may have a similar statute or you may consider gathering support to have legislation passed.

O.C.G.A. § 40-6-6 entitled, "Authorized emergency vehicles," covers several topics, everything from what constitutes an emergency vehicle to the obligations placed upon the operator of an emergency vehicle. For our purposes, we will look at the following sections of this statute:

(d)(1) The foregoing provisions shall not relieve the driver of an authorized emergency vehicle from the duty to drive with due regard for the safety of all persons.

(2) When a law enforcement officer in a law enforcement vehicle is pursuing a fleeing suspect in another vehicle and the fleeing suspect damages any property or injures or kills any person during the pursuit, the law enforcement officer's pursuit shall not be the proximate cause or a contributing proximate cause of the damage, injury, or death caused by the fleeing suspect *unless the law enforcement officer acted with reckless disregard for proper law enforcement procedures* in the officer's *decision to initiate or continue the pursuit. Where such reckless disregard exists, the pursuit may be found to constitute a proximate cause of the damage, injury, or death caused by the fleeing suspect, but the existence*

of such reckless disregard shall not in and of itself establish causation.

(3) The provisions of this subsection shall apply only to issues of causation and duty and shall not affect the existence or absence of immunity which shall be determined as otherwise provided by law. (Emphasis added).

As you can see from the language of the statute, the law provides for some immunity to LEOs during pursuits, outlines the parameters of that immunity, and sets forth the analysis to be used by courts interpreting the statute. Keep in mind that this statute points to "proper law enforcement procedures." This means you will be judged by your peers and not just the policy of the agency. This is the exact type of information that an expert witness will provide to a jury.

Sections of the statute cited above, O.C.G.A. § 40-6-6, "was a legislative response to the Georgia Supreme Court's decision in *Mixon v. City of Warner Robins.* 260 Ga. 385 (1994). In the *Mixon* case, the Georgia Supreme Court held that police officers could be held civilly liable for injuries sustained by an innocent third party if the officer's decision to initiate and continue a pursuit was performed without "due regard for the safety of all persons[81]." This liability could extend to situations in which the injury was actually inflicted by the fleeing suspect.[82]" 12 Ga. St. U. L. Rev. 295, 295 (1996) (Internal citations omitted).

---

[81] 264 Ga. 385, 387 (1994).
[82] Id.

As is often the case with legislation, a group of people came together and presented a bill to the legislature to change the law. The goal was to protect LEOs, agencies and governments from lawsuits involving vehicle pursuits stemming from injuries to innocent third parties caused by the perpetrator.

In 2011, the Georgia Court of Appeals interpreted the immunity portion of this statute. This is important for LEOs, as the first few courts to interpret a statute provide important information and guidance for LEOs who must comply with the law as interpreted by the courts. This is, in part, the analysis of "clearly established law" examined by the USSC in the cases of qualified immunity discussed above.

The Georgia Court of Appeals issued an opinion in the case of *Strength v. Lovett*, 311 Ga. App. 35 (2011) on Nov. 30, 2011. The case lists the comment "cert. denied" which means that the Georgia Supreme Court declined to hear or review the case. Therefore, this is the final decision for this case. While courts are clear that no inference can be drawn when a court declined to review a case, it is important to note that the Georgia Supreme Court did not feel the decision of the Georgia Court of Appeals warranted review.

In *Strength v. Lovett*, the Georgia Court of Appeals reviewed a case wherein a Richmond County Deputy started a pursuit of a young driver. The pursuit reached high speeds quickly and ended quickly when the driver hit a car that was not involved in the pursuit, killing a passenger in that car. The passenger's estate and children brought suit against Ronnie Strength, the Sheriff of Richmond County, in his official capacity, alleging that the deputy, when he chose to continue the pursuit even after it reached high speeds, acted in reckless disregard of proper police procedures and thereby caused the passenger's death. The Sheriff moved for summary judgment, asserting both sovereign immunity and that the plaintiffs could not prove that the choice of the deputy to continue the pursuit was a legal cause of the passenger's death. The trial court denied the motion for summary judgment, and the Sheriff appealed. The Court of Appeals vacated the order denying the motion and remanded the case to the lower court to consider whether the plaintiffs had sufficient evidence to create a jury question on the issue of cause in fact. The Court of Appeals found no error in the court's denial of summary judgment on sovereign immunity and proximate cause grounds. It is important to note that the deputy was still able to seek dismissal on the grounds of qualified immunity.

In the final analysis of lawsuits v. reality, it is important to note that a violation of departmental policy does not necessarily mean that you will lose the civil case or that you will not be entitled to qualified immunity. While you should always strive to stay within departmental policy, this is an important principle to understand and possibly explain to the attorney representing you. In *Fennell v. Gilstrap*, the Eleventh Circuit stated,

> A jailor's use of force against a pretrial detainee is excessive under the Fourteenth Amendment if it "shocks the conscience." The use of force does not "shock the conscience" if it is applied "in a good-faith effort to maintain or restore discipline." However, if the force is applied "maliciously and sadistically to cause harm," then it does

"shock the conscience," and is excessive under the Eighth or Fourteenth Amendments[83].

The standard for showing excessive force in violation of the Fourteenth Amendment, therefore, is higher than that required to show excessive force in violation of the Fourth Amendment. *And, indeed, it is higher than that required to show excessive force in violation of Bartow County Sheriff's Office's policies. Here, the Bartow County Sheriff's Office, after an internal investigation, concluded that Gilstrap's use of force was both excessive and unnecessary. That conclusion, even if correct, does not answer the question of whether Gilstrap maliciously and sadistically used force to cause Fennell harm, and thus violated Fennell's Fourteenth Amendment rights.*

We *consider the following factors in determining whether the force was applied maliciously and sadistically to cause harm, and thus violated the Fourteenth Amendment:* a) the need for the application of force; b) the relationship between the need and the amount of force that was used; c) the extent of the injury inflicted upon the prisoner; d) the extent of the threat to the safety of staff and inmates; and e) any efforts made to temper the severity of a forceful response. []

---

[83] Eighth Amendment decisional law is applicable to Fourteenth Amendment claims. This was a case involving an inmate. In these cases, the courts apply the standard of the Eighth Amendment not the Fourth Amendment. *Fennell v. Gilstrap*, 559 F.3d 1212 (11th Cir. 2009).

When considering these factors, *we "give a wide range of deference to prison officials acting to preserve discipline and security, including when considering decisions made at the scene of a disturbance."* We examine the facts as reasonably perceived by Gilstrap on the basis of the facts known to him at the time. *Fennell v. Gilstrap*, 559 F.3d 1212, 1217-18 (11th Cir. 2009). (Internal citations omitted). (Emphasis added).

This standard bears repeating. The factors to be considered are:

1. The need for the application of force.
2. The relationship between the need and the amount of force that was used.
3. The extent of the injury inflicted upon the prisoner.
4. The extent of the threat to the safety of staff and inmates.
5. Any efforts made to temper the severity of a forceful response.

It also bears repeating that the courts will "examine the facts as reasonably perceived by [law enforcement officers] on the basis of the facts known to him at the time[84]." Finally, it is important to note that the policies of the law enforcement agency do not represent the final criteria of the excessive force analysis. In fact, Deputy Gilstrap was

---

[84] *Fennell v. Gilstrap*, 559 F.3d 1212 (11th Cir. 2009).

fired from his agency but the Eleventh Circuit afforded him qualified immunity and dismissed the civil case against him finding that his actions were within the law. Discipline from the agency and winning or losing a civil suit are separate and distinct analyses.

CHAPTER EIGHT
THE STATE LICENSING INVESTIGATION

I'm not afraid of much, but I'm afraid of POST.
I'm scared to death of POST.

–LEO client who requested to remain
anonymous

Every state has an agency that certifies, licenses, or issues a commission to LEOs. For ease of discussion, I will use the term "certify." While the name of the agency varies, the mission is the same—set minimum criteria for eligibility, training, initial certification, and continuing certification. Each agency also has a duty and the authority to regulate the conduct of those who are certified as LEOs. This includes the obligation to investigate allegations of misconduct and assess the eligibility of a person to remain certified as a peace officer. In Georgia, this agency is the Peace Officers Standards and Training Council (POST). For ease of discussion, I will refer to this agency as POST throughout this chapter[85]. I will also use state law and rules and regulations of the State of Georgia as examples.

This is not a concept unique to LEOs. Every state has a similar agency for the certification of physicians, nurses, surveyors, architects, and many other professionals. POST has the authority to investigate misconduct of those who hold a certification under its jurisdiction. In many cases, POST investigators are peace officers who are authorized to take arrest warrants and seek search warrants. False statements to these investigators constitute crimes. Their mission is to protect the public, maintain the public trust, and ensure professional standards.

On the "entry" side of the certification process, POST must have the ability to investigate the statements and representations made by applicants seeking certification.

---

[85] Seventeen states (AL, AZ, CA, CO, CT, GA, ID, KS, LA, MN, MO, MS, ND, NV, TN, UT, WY) refer to the certifying agency as POST in some form. The corresponding agency in Texas is known as the Commission on Law Enforcement Standards and Education, Illinois' agency is known as the Law Enforcement Training and Standards Board, and Ohio LEOs are regulated by the Peace Officer Training Commission.

For example, a candidate seeking to enter the mandate[86] academy (police academy) can be prosecuted for any false statements made in connection with the application process and may be excluded from certification based upon psychiatric disorders, drug or alcohol addiction, or prior criminal conduct.

Once a person is certified by POST, that entity has jurisdiction over the person to investigate allegations of misconduct and determine if the person remains fit to continue in the profession[87]. This inquiry usually begins with a report to the POST of misconduct, alleged misconduct, or a change in employment status by the law enforcement agency that employs the LEO[88]. LEOs are also required to "self-report" arrests, violations of federal, state, or local law, mental incompetence, and addiction to drugs or alcohol[89]. It should also be noted that LEOs may be

---

[86] This is the entry level training for basic certification as a sworn LEO in Georgia. Other states use different terms.

[87] POST has jurisdiction and authority to refuse to grant a certificate to or to discipline a certified peace officer or an exempt peace officer under this chapter or any antecedent law. O.C.G.A. § 35-8-7.

[88] Ga Comp. R. & Regs. 464-3-.06.

[89] Any applicant/candidate for certification or person certified pursuant to O.C.G.A. Title 35, Chapter 8, who has disciplinary action taken against him/ her by any agency, organ, or department of this State, a subdivision or municipality thereof, or federal, shall notify the Council within fifteen (15) days of said action. For purposes of the fifteen (15) day time limit, evidence that notification was mailed within fifteen (15) days shall be sufficient. Disciplinary action as used herein means any action taken by any municipal, county, state or federal agency against a certified officer, which meet any of the following criteria:

(a) arrest by local, state, or federal authorities;

(b) suspensions, in totality, of thirty (30) days or longer for singular incidents of misconduct, demotions (other than for administrative purposes), termination by employing agency, or resignations in lieu of terminations;

(c) indictments or presentments in any local, state or federal courts;

(d) conviction or bond forfeiture, in any local, state or federal court. The term "conviction" shall include a finding or verdict of guilt, plea of guilty, or a plea of nolo contendere, regardless of whether the adjudication of guilt or sentence is withheld or not entered thereon;

allowed to continue their employment when substance abuse and addiction is self-reported to POST. I strongly urge any LEO to seek the cooperation of POST when they seek treatment. You will generally find a group of individuals who will work with you to set in place a program that may allow you to remain certified. This is the case with most licensing agencies for other professions as well.

For Georgia LEOs, the authority of POST to regulate our profession is found in Title 35 of the Official Code of Georgia. Each state will have a statute that creates the agency that regulates and investigates LEOs. This is known as enabling legislation. There will be other statutes that set out the power, jurisdiction, and authority of the regulatory agency. You will also find rules and regulations of the state agency. Developed and adopted by the agency, these regulations formally and clearly set out the authority, the standards enforced, and the procedures followed as they execute their mission. I will cite to these rules throughout this chapter, and many times include the citations and excerpts in the footnotes so that you may see examples. All states will follow a similar pattern. The legislature will establish the regulatory agency and the agency will adopt the rules and regulations necessary to accomplish its mission.

For example, in Georgia, the main statute to consider in this discussion is O.C.G.A. §35-8-7.1. The full text of this code section can be found in the reference section. For our purposes, the following portions are most important:

(e) minor traffic citations written to a certified officer need not be reported to the Council.
Ga. Comp. R. & Regs. 464-3-.05

(a) The council shall have authority to refuse to grant a certificate to an applicant *or to discipline a certified peace officer* or exempt peace officer under this chapter or any antecedent law upon a determination by the council that the applicant or certified peace officer or exempt peace officer has:

...

(2) Knowingly made misleading, deceptive, untrue, or fraudulent representations *in the practice of being a peace officer* or in *any document connected therewith* or *practiced fraud or deceit* or intentionally made any false statement in obtaining a certificate to practice as a peace officer[90];

(3) Been *convicted of a felony in the courts of this state or any other state, territory, country, or of the United States.* As used in this paragraph, the term "conviction of a felony" shall include a conviction of an offense which if committed in this state would be deemed a felony under either state or federal law without regard to its designation elsewhere. As used in this paragraph, the term "conviction" shall include a finding or a verdict of guilt, a plea of guilty, or a plea of nolo contendere in a criminal proceeding, regardless of whether the adjudication of guilt or sentence is withheld or not entered thereon. However, the council may not

---

[90] Any untrue, misleading, or omitted statement contained in any such application shall be cause for denial, and if any registration has been granted, it shall be cause for the revocation of same. Ga. Comp. R. & Regs. 464-3-.01

deny a certificate to an applicant with a conviction if the adjudication of guilt or sentence is withheld or not entered thereon;

(4) *Committed a crime involving moral turpitude[91], without regard to conviction.* The conviction of a crime involving moral turpitude shall be conclusive of the commission of such crime. As used in this paragraph, the term "conviction" shall have the meaning prescribed in paragraph (3) of this subsection;

(5) Had his certificate or license to practice as a peace officer revoked, suspended, or annulled by any lawful certifying or licensing authority; or had other disciplinary action taken against him by any lawful certifying or licensing authority; or was denied a certificate or license by any lawful certifying or licensing authority;

(6) *Engaged in any unprofessional, unethical, deceptive, or deleterious conduct or practice harmful to the public,* which conduct or practice need not have resulted in actual injury to any person. As used in this paragraph, the term "unprofessional conduct" shall include *any departure from, or failure to conform to, the minimal standards of acceptable and prevailing practice of a peace officer;*

---

[91] As used in Georgia, moral turpitude seems to mean infamy. One of the earlier cases on the subject, *Ford v. State*, after reciting the rule, said: "Evidence which discredits a witness on the ground of infamy tends to impeach him." Basically, it would seem that any crime designated as a felony and punishable by imprisonment would be a crime involving moral turpitude within the meaning of the law. Felonies are infamous. *Lewis v. State*, 243 Ga. 443, 445, 254 S.E.2d 830, 832 (1979). (Internal citations omitted).

(7) *Violated or attempted to violate a law, rule, or regulation of this state, any other state, the council, the United States, or any other lawful authority without regard to whether the violation is criminally punishable, which law, rule, or regulation relates to or in part regulates the practice of a peace officer;*

(8) *Committed any act or omission which is indicative of bad moral character or untrustworthiness;*

(9) *Been adjudged mentally incompetent by a court of competent jurisdiction,* within or outside this state;

(10) *Become unable to perform as a peace officer with reasonable skill and safety to citizens by reason of illness or use of alcohol, drugs, narcotics, chemicals, or any other type of material or as a result of any mental or physical condition;* or

(11) *Been suspended or discharged* by the peace officer's employing law enforcement unit for disciplinary reasons.

POST has the authority to obtain documents and information necessary to perform investigations pursuant to the law, without permission or a waiver of privacy from the LEO[92]. The question of whether POST can obtain any and all medical records in compliance with the Health Insurance Portability and Accountability Act (HIPAA) is

---

[92] The Council shall have the authority to initiate inquiries to determine compliance with the Peace Officer Standards and Training Act by an individual officer or employing agency of State and local government. *The officer's waiver signed upon application shall authorize the Council to obtain documents and other information necessary for the inquiry.* Ga. Comp. R. & Regs. 464-3-.07. (Emphasis added).

not settled. However, a LEO will likely bear the burden of establishing a justification to conceal such medical records from a POST investigation when the treatment is relevant. This is also the case with pilots, nurses, physicians, and other licensed professionals. Consult an attorney before ever refusing to provide documents to POST during an investigation[93]. Further, the protections afforded to statements made to in an administrative investigation, which I described in Chapter Five, may not apply to an investigation by POST[94]. Because POST does not have the ability to terminate your employment, the protections under Garrity may not attach. This is an unsettled area of the law.

The activities of a licensing agency are governed by an area of the law known as Administrative Law. There are several important considerations regarding administrative law that are relevant to our discussion. First, administrative law generally relates to the statutory authority of the agency to regulate LEOs. Second, the agency has the authority to establish rules and regulations that will be adopted by the state to govern the activities of the agency. Third, the agency has the ability to "prosecute" violations of the statutes, rules, and regulations. Finally, the deadlines and the procedures outlined in the statutes and rules and regulations are strict, hard deadlines. For example, when a LEO has a set amount of time to appeal a proposed discipline, a failure to properly file an appeal within the time allotted will generally forfeit the right to challenge the proposed action, have a hearing, or present

---

[93]...refusal to cooperate amounted to unprofessional conduct sufficient to justify decertification."*GA POST Council v. Anderson*, 290 Ga. App. 91, 94, 658 S.E.2d 840, 843 (2008).
[94] *GA POST Council v. Anderson*, 290 Ga. App. 91, 94, 658 S.E.2d 840, 843 (2008).

evidence in opposition to the proposed action. Further, the proposed action will become the official action and there is little that the LEO can do to change that result.

Administrative proceedings in Georgia are governed by the Administrative Procedures Act[95]. The act sets forth how cases are handled by state licensing agencies, how decisions are appealed, and how an agency enforces sanctions. Your state likely has a similar statute. Although it may be interesting to read, the act is more geared as a procedural tool for attorneys handling these cases.

Whenever an action is taken by POST, the LEO must be notified to comply with the due process rights secured by the United States Constitution and state constitutions. This is accomplished in many ways. In Georgia, POST is authorized to provide notice in person or through certified mail[96]. In 2011, POST updated and enhanced their website to allow LEOs to update their address to ensure they will receive timely notification of investigations and proposed actions. The LEO, as an individual, is required to ensure that the training records and address on file with POST are current, and must update this information within thirty days of any change[97]. Law enforcement agencies are

---

[95] O.C.G.A. § 50-13-1, et seq.

[96] The Council shall notify all officers by mail or hand delivery of any disciplinary action or a hearing to determine if disciplinary action is appropriate. For purposes of notification, mailing by delivery confirmation or certified mail to the last address specified on the application or the last known address of the officer shall constitute proper service. Ga. Comp. R. & Regs. 464-3-.08.

[97] All registration applications under these Rules shall be a permanent record. It is expressly made the responsibility of the registered officer to keep such application current. Should any change occur during subsequent years after registration which would require a different answer to any questions contained in the application, or supporting document which is made a part of the application, such change must be reported as an amendment to the application within thirty (30) days of the date of the occurrence of such change. Ga. Comp. R. & Regs. 464-4-.03

required to notify POST within fifteen days of any change in employment status[98].

Notice to the LEO of any proposed action against his certification is part of the due process afforded by the federal and state constitutions[99]. Remember that due process consists of notice and an opportunity to be heard[100]. In administrative law terms, your failure to submit a timely and proper response to a notification from a certifying agency within the time allowed by law means you have forfeited your right to be heard. However, the agency bears the burden of proving it has properly provided notice to the LEO, and a failure to provide proper notice will invalidate any action taken by the agency[101].

I have met with many LEOs who failed to respond in a timely manner to a POST investigation. In nearly every case, there was little that I could do to help them. One exception may be when the sole reason a LEO fails to respond is that she was deployed as a reservist in the United States Armed Forces. In that case, the Soldiers' and Sailors' Civil Relief Act of 1940[102] may provide some assistance. However, you should involve an attorney before petitioning POST for relief under these circumstances.

---

[98] Hiring, promotions, termination of employment and other changes in the employment status of a registered officer is the responsibility of the agency to report within fifteen (15) days of the occurrence of such change in status. Ga. Comp. R. & Regs. 464-4-.03

[99] " . . .nor shall any State deprive any person of life, liberty, or property, without due process of law." U.S. Const. amend. XIV, § 1; No person shall be deprived of life, liberty, or property except by due process of law. Ga. Const. art. I, § 1, ¶ I

[100] "The fundamental idea of due process is notice and an opportunity to be heard. *Hood v. Carsten*, 267 Ga. 579, 580, 481 S.E.2d 525, 527 (1997)

[101] *Mitsubishi Motors Credit of America, Inc. v. Robinson & Stephens, Inc.*, 263 Ga.App. 168, 587 S.E.2d 146 (2003) reconsideration denied, certiorari denied, on remand.

[102] 50 App. U.S.C.A. § 524.

When POST becomes involved in an investigation, it has many options available in response to allegations or proof of misconduct. POST can elect not to take any action and find the discipline taken by the law enforcement agency was sufficient. POST can also mandate training, require treatment for substance abuse or mental health issues, place a LEO on probation, administer a reprimand, limit a certificate, suspend a LEO, or revoke a certification[103]. In Georgia, a LEO may petition to regain her certification after a period of two years[104].

In the event of a felony arrest or any other action that poses a threat to the public, POST has the authority to immediately issue an emergency suspension of the certificate pending a hearing[105]. In the event of such action, known as a summary suspension, POST must provide for a timely hearing for the LEO to challenge the suspension.

In 2011, the Georgia General Assembly imposed additional notification requirements on POST. POST is now required to notify the law enforcement agency via priority mail when POST initiates an investigation of a LEO or imposes discipline upon a LEO. POST is also required to notify the law enforcement agency if the investigation is closed without action[106]. Further, if the certification of the LEO is suspended or revoked, POST is now required to notify, via priority mail, the head of the law enforcement agency, the district attorney of the jurisdiction, and the solicitor general of the state court, if applicable[107].

---

[103] O.C.G.A. § 35-8-7.1(b)(1)(A-F)
[104] Ga Comp. R. & Regs. 464-18-.01.
[105] O.C.G.A. § 35-8-7.1(d)
[106] O.C.G.A. § 35-8-7.1(e)
[107] O.C.G.A. § 35-8-7.1(f)

POST also has the authority to mandate annual training. In Georgia, LEOs are required to obtain twenty annual hours of training. If a LEO fails to obtain the required number of hours, she will lose her power of arrest[108]. Further, this annual training must include qualification with a firearm and use of force training, to include one hour of training specifically related to the use of deadly force[109].

By now, you may have realized just how important it is to properly handle and respond to an administrative investigation. You may also see how important it is to get an attorney involved to assist you early-on in the process. You have a right to counsel at every stage of the process, and an attorney can assist in preparing statements, gathering documents, and negotiating with POST if necessary to obtain an appropriate outcome. If you are forced to pursue appeals through a hearing before the POST council or appeal a decision of the POST council, it would be foolish to proceed without an attorney. You have too much at stake. The Legal Defense Plan through the Fraternal Order of Police will provide an attorney to assist you with administrative actions.

It is important to keep in mind that the state licensing investigation may lag behind the criminal and administrative investigations because your agency will likely wait to report any misconduct or discipline to POST until after its investigation and disciplinary process is complete. In addition, the state licensing investigation may also take place in the midst of a civil case. The critical point is that

---

[108] " . . .any person employed or appointed as a peace officer shall complete twenty hours of training as provided in this Code section . . . Any peace officer who does not fulfill the training requirements of this Code section shall lose his power of arrest. Ga. Code Ann. § 35-8-21(a)&(d).

[109] Ga Comp. R. & Regs. 464-5-.03.1

you should keep your attorney informed of the status of all investigations. This is especially true when you are required to provide statements or documents. While it may surprise you, the state licensing investigation is independent from the other investigations and is not bound by the outcome of those inquiries. For example, following a shooting, a LEO could be cleared by a grand jury but be subject to sanction by POST. Likewise, a settlement in a civil case may have no effect upon your certification. This logically follows from the mission of POST to regulate the profession.

If you receive a notice from POST indicating that you are under investigation or that POST is taking action against your certification, remember the following important steps:

1. Write down the date and time that you were made aware of the investigation or proposed action.

2. Write down the date and time that you were served with or received any documentation from POST regarding the investigation or proposed action.

3. READ THE LETTER and all documents you receive.

4. Determine when you are required to respond and note the response deadlines on your calendar with reminders three days before the deadlines.

5. Determine whether you are required to respond by letter, by phone, or in person.

6. Contact an attorney as soon as possible, preferably the day you receive the documentation from POST.

7. Gather any documents or materials in your possession that you believe will assist you and your attorney.

8. Make a list of any documents, materials, or witnesses that you believe may assist you or your attorney.

9. Keep the fact of the investigation or proposed action quiet unless you are required to notify your chain of command, or unless you are told by POST that your certification is immediately suspended or revoked.

10. Meet with the attorney you choose as soon as possible and cooperate fully with her efforts to assist you.

The state licensing agency is the standard bearer for the law enforcement profession within your state. Every profession must have standards and an independent body charged with setting and maintaining those standards. If we are to continue to promote law enforcement as a profession, we must not only cooperate with the efforts of POST, but also support the role of POST as the men and women of that agency perform their assigned duties. You can show your support by learning the rules and the requirements placed upon you as a LEO. Satisfy your obligations by meeting the deadlines outlined in the law, and seek counsel early in the event of an investigation or proposed sanction. You will find that in the overwhelming majority of cases, the licensing agency will fairly evaluate and adjudicate the matters before it. In the final analysis, we are all better off because of its efforts.

CHAPTER NINE
THE SPOUSE AND FAMILY

Q: Do you recall who had called you?

A: I thought it was [my husband] calling me because he had called me previously in the evening to let me know that he was going to serve one more warrant and he should be home on time. So I thought he was calling to tell me that he was wrapping things up and getting ready to leave work. When I answered the phone the lady mispronounced my name and then told me she was the head nurse at North Fulton Hospital.

Q: Do you recall the substance of her conversation to you at that time?

A: I believe that as soon as she told me she was the head nurse at North Fulton Hospital, I jumped out of the bed and she said that my husband had told her to tell me to not go crazy and to try to relax that he had been in an altercation and that they had brought him to the Emergency Room. And I said, "Okay" and she said he had been shot in the chest.

— Deposition testimony of a wife of a LEO during a civil suit against the estate of the man who shot her husband

Good or bad, if something happens to you, it affects your family and friends. Think of your excitement when you were hired as a LEO, when you graduated the academy, and when you made your first felony arrest. You shared those good times with the people closest to you. They celebrated your accomplishments, encouraged you to push hard toward continued success, and looked forward to the next milestone in your career.

The people who stood by and encouraged you in the good times also will be there for you in the trying times. This is part of the relationship. Just as you rush to the side of a friend who loses a parent or is injured in a car wreck, the people close to you will experience the effects and stresses of an OIS. Many times it is harder for them than for you.

We all enjoy the sense of being in control of our lives. People generally believe their actions and thoughts make a difference. We go to sleep at night, wake up in the morning, and get through the day focused on making things better for ourselves, those around us, and those we care about. However, unexpected, uncontrollable events occur. This fact can increase the stress of those events exponentially. This is especially true when misfortune or injury occurs to someone we love.

Think about it from this perspective. Although they may not ever complain about it, your spouse and loved ones have no control over what happens to you while you are on duty as a LEO. They may help you get some sleep or assist in your efforts to become better trained and physically fit. However, once you put on your uniform and leave the house, all they can do is hope and pray for your safe return. Such is the life of your family, every shift and every day throughout your career.

Within minutes, there were a couple more people back there with me, to make sure I was okay. All I really wanted to do at that time, the only thing I wanted to do was talk to my wife; that was it. When I heard her voice, I was overwhelmed. Of course, she was watching it all on TV. You can still see it's emotional.

–Name withheld

When you are involved in a critical incident, your family will see the effects when you return home. They will watch as you go through the investigations, the media scrutiny[110], and the efforts you make to return to normal. You must expect that your sleepless nights, mood swings, and fears will have an effect on them. However, in many ways it is worse for them because they have no context in which to understand what you are going through, and there is little, if anything, they can do but be supportive and hope that you return to your "old self." This may be the case even if you are married to or dating another LEO.

Many LEOs do not think about a frequent side effect of being involved in a critical incident—financial difficulties. I have represented LEOs who were not permitted to work part-time or extra jobs for as long as eighteen months after an OIS. This put a tremendous financial strain on these LEOs and their families. In one case, the LEO was forced to leave his chosen profession because he was unable to support his family without those part-time jobs.

---

[110] As I stated earlier in this book, you and your family should avoid all media coverage of the OIS or critical incident.

Hopefully, you now understand that your spouse and family will need outside support, just as you will, after a critical incident. The good news is that there are many resources and many good people ready and willing to help. These people and organizations give their time, resources, and in many cases money, to help LEOs through these tough times. Many of these groups work with LEOs who are injured, or families who lose a loved one. Know that many stand by ready to assist you or your family in any way possible. Remarkably, they ask for little in return.

The Fraternal Order of Police, the Fraternal Order of Police Auxiliary, Wives Behind the Badge, Inc, the Golden Shield, Concerns of Police Survivors, thousands of police chaplains, including Too Small A Thing (www.scottyhdavis.com), the Christian Police Association (www.cpa-usa.org), Critical Incident Stress Management (www.cismperspectives.com), and many other associations offer assistance to LEOs and their families to help cope with the stress of a critical incident. If you think this is a long list of resources, think again. I could not possibly list all of the resources, groups, societies, and individuals who stand ready, willing, and able to support you and your family. They stand for you because you stand for what is right.

One LEO I represented in an OIS watched as his seven year old son brought his toy guns into his parents' bedroom where my client was about to take a nap. When asked what he was doing, the boy replied, "I'll watch for the bad guys while you sleep, Daddy." Reach out to these people and groups and let them help you and the ones you love. There is no reason for you or your family to go through this stress alone.

CHAPTER TEN
GOING FORWARD

When I was in the police Academy, one of the instructors poured three quarters of a gallon of red Kool-Aid on the ground and said, 'Unless you see this much blood on the ground, you are not going to die.' After I was shot, I did not see a lot of blood, so I knew I was going to survive.

Chris was shot at close range with a .357 magnum revolver loaded with hollow point bullets while serving a misdemeanor shoplifting warrant. The bullet entered his chest between the panels of his vest, traversed his body and exited high on his left chest. All of the blood stayed inside his chest and Chris saw no blood. The suspect took his own life during a stand-off.

Chris Lee is still serving with the Cobb County Sheriff's Office.

One of my favorite TV detectives said he got through tough times in his life by looking forward to the next sunrise. For me, no truer words have been spoken. I am often amazed at how people survive the hardships they face. As I write this, one of my friends is recovering from a stroke. Through sheer determination, faith in God, strength from family and friends, or a combination of all of these factors, people seem to prove every day how we cannot underestimate the resilience of the human spirit.

Part of going forward is being prepared for what may or may not happen. Everything is easier when you are prepared for the task. While I would love to tell you the road forward will be smooth, that is most often not the case. The fact is that many LEOs involved in an OIS face anxiety, depression, and insomnia and are at risk for substance abuse, marital strife, and suicide. We can try to wish away the effects of a critical incident or prepare now to handle the alligators as we walk through the swamp. I prefer the latter.

> *The use of deadly force is very different in the military. You expect to engage the enemy and return to your base at the end of the patrol. You get something to eat, grab some sleep and go out again to engage the enemy as necessary. You prepare to receive fire and get wounded. Law enforcement is different. You expect the routine day and the use of force is, to a large extent, unexpected.*
>
> -Former LEO and retired Army Special Forces soldier

I have never spoken with a LEO at the scene of an OIS prior to an administrative interview or after a lawsuit was filed who said, "This upcoming interview and potential lawsuit are nothing. I am worried about the national statistics regarding the number of LEOs who suffer from insomnia!" After a critical incident, most, if not all, LEOs are focused on whether they should have a lawyer when they speak with investigators, their rights in a criminal investigation, and whether the agency will defend them in a lawsuit. However, the information in this chapter is, in my opinion, more important than interviews and administrative actions. While you may define yourself as a LEO, your life is comprised of much more than your career.

What You Can and Should Expect From your Agency

Most, if not all, agencies will allow a LEO time off on paid administrative leave. While the time varies from a few days to two weeks, the LEO usually must stay in town absent special permission. This time should be spent getting rest and reassuring your spouse and children that you are OK while taking the time to work through the effects of the critical incident. The most important thing to remember is this is *your* time. You have a support system in friends, family, and church that will shore you up *if* you seek their help.

I have run into situations where LEOs were new to town or single, and wanted to return home to see their family and pastor. In these situations, explain the circumstances to your chain of command. Generally, as long as you are available by phone during the day, spending time in your home or with family out of state will have no effect on the agency or the investigation. In one case, a LEO client of mine was offered a few days away with his family at a vacation home at no charge. His chain of command approved. The trip was just what the LEO and his family needed. They were also able to escape relentless, uninformed official and unofficial media attention.

One final piece of advice that bears repeating during this time: ignore the media. You were there. You do not need to watch the news to find out what happened. Even with the best of intentions, media outlets will not have all of the facts. The media world is filled with "experts" who are more than willing to criticize and second guess your decisions. Listening to them is not productive and may prove very harmful. This goes for any other "experts" in your family, agency, or community who have advice on how things should have been done.

Your agency likely has an employee assistance program (EAP) that provides counseling at no charge. Many agencies provide this service for LEOs and their spouses. This is different from any evaluation set up by the agency for the LEO. In many states, the privacy of sessions with EAP is not as secure as in other states. I encourage LEOs and their families to seek out a private counselor or psychiatrist and use their health insurance to pay for it if extended and personal counseling is recommended or desired. This is especially true if the counseling will extend to issues beyond the OIS. In this scenario, the statements made to the counselor or psychiatrist are more likely to be held confidential. After all, the stress of the critical incident could bring out more issues than the shooting. Protect your privacy, but do not be afraid to seek help.

Your agency will likely send you for an evaluation by a licensed counselor or psychiatrist. This is more on the order of a fitness for duty evaluation, but is standard practice throughout the United States. The counselor or psychiatrist will usually meet with you soon after the incident and perhaps several times before you return to work. The goal of this professional is to ensure that you are appropriately responding to the stress of the critical incident. Notice I said "appropriately responding." It may be perfectly normal for you to experience insomnia, nightmares, episodes of crying, or being overprotective of yourself and family. However, it is also normal for these effects to pass with time.

At some point, the counselor wants to know that you are through the tough parts and ready to return to the "normal stress" associated with being a LEO. Remember that these sessions should be focused on the critical incident. As stated above, there is a limitation on the confidentiality of information you provide during these sessions.

You can also expect a day at the firing range and likely the simulator. After an OIS, it is critical to get the LEO back on the range to shoot. Firing a weapon involves far more than noise. There is recoil, a shockwave to the shooter, the smell of gunpowder, the sound of the brass hitting the ground, and the vision of the rounds hitting the target. Many LEOs "hear" the shots for the first time after an OIS when the go to the firing range. The effects of auditory exclusion are so strong that the LEO may have a large gap in his memory about the event. Firearms trainers must be trained to look for signs of extreme stress during these sessions. The LEO must work through these issues. Firearms simulator systems that utilize flashing lights, low light situations, and sound can also be very beneficial. Make no mistake—the agency is also trying to protect itself and other LEOs in the event of another shooting. They must make certain that the LEO is able to use deadly force following an OIS. If you believe you will have difficulty meeting agency standards, or if your marksmanship skills are marginal, make certain you get enough practice prior to any attempt to requalify with your service weapons.

You can and also should expect a support system complete with chaplains, friends willing to listen and provide support in the form of food, child care, or, in some cases, money to cover the extra jobs you will not be able to work for a while. The Fraternal Order of Police, including the Auxiliary, will be there to help if you are a member. My advice: take their help. Do not be shy. You are just like anyone else and could use some extra support during this time. Further, you would not hesitate to help another LEO in this way. Sometimes we show our strength by admitting we need support and allowing others to help.

When Words Hurt More Than Bullets

In the course of writing this book and throughout my careers, I have run into LEOs who experienced some extreme ridicule. Some came from the press, some from the public, but the worst and most damaging came from within their own departments. I've interviewed LEOs, some of whom are not quoted in this book, who experienced what can only be described as horrible experiences after an OIS or other critical incident. For many reasons, this practice must cease and we must all be vigilant to stop it.

> *When I came back to work, everybody was wonderful to me. It never came up among the officers. It seemed like I may have started running into issues with the supervisors.*
>
> –Name withheld

Some LEOs are teased about their performance when their tactics are second guessed. Others face incessant critique when a suspect survives a shooting. Still others are treated differently by beat partners and supervisors who are concerned about the LEO who "went through something like that." Perhaps this is one of the reasons why many LEOs leave the profession after a critical incident. I have spoken to more than one LEO who nearly took his own life because he could not escape the harassment and felt like the one group that had his back at all times had turned on him.

> *Since my shooting, I've been able to reach out to others who have been through this. You know, it's one thing to recognize a critical incident that somebody's gone through and another thing to do something about it. And it's not just shootings. I realized after my incident there was a guy at our department who was having a tough time doing his job and I got to thinking about some things he had gone through. He got bitten by a dog and had some pretty severe injuries. He got attacked on a warrant pull and everybody screwed with him about that when he came back to work. People are cruel and they don't realize they are. Some of the things they say, some of the*

stupid questions they ask, some of the stupid comments they make, those things dig deep.

−Name withheld

The off-handed quip in a squad room or the "running joke" can strike hard at the LEO who is working through the stress of any critical incident. We cannot afford to be the cause of destruction in the life of any LEO in any way at any time. Supervisors MUST intervene and stop the destructive forces before they grow. They must also lead by example.

When Not All the LEOs Involved in the Critical Incident Return to Duty

The best advice I got was from another officer, I won't name him but he was involved in a shooting. "He, he told me, 'You're okay now. It's not going to hit you for a couple months.'

−Name withheld

In movies, books, and television stories of OISs, there is one good guy and one bad guy. The bad guy does something...well..."bad," and the good guy shoots and kills him. This set of facts goes back to stories of the Wild West and gunfights in the streets. Perhaps there are two good guys or more than one bad guy, but the outcome is always the same: the bad guy dies and the good guys win and live happily ever after. Real life is not a movie or a novel. Sometimes, the good guys do not go home. Other times, the good guys go home, but never return to work.

LEOs are sworn to perform a dangerous job. In service to the public, we take risks. Despite the occasional complaints in the squad room, we love our profession and work each day to serve with pride. LEOs know all too well that dedication may lead one of our brothers or sisters to lose their life or suffer an injury that changes their life forever.

Survivors of critical incidents have often prepared for the use of deadly force. Through training, classes, and personal preparation, many LEOs go to great efforts to ensure their survival. However, sometimes, the good guys do not escape unharmed. From evacuating wounded LEOs from the field of fire to the administration of first aid, the prospect that one of your friends and coworkers may be injured must be part of your training. After you are safe, the threat is gone, and the crime scene tape is up, the process of going forward is so much harder when a LEO is injured.

> *It's never going to leave your mind. It's no– it becomes–it moves from something you dwell on to something that passes through your mind every day. Over time it becomes just a subconscious thing. It just runs through and you don't pay attention to it anymore but it's there, it's always running around.*
>
> –Name withheld

If a LEO is killed in the line of duty, the community embraces the agency and the family. There are many resources available to help including benefit programs, education and scholarships for the survivors, and memorial programs to remember their sacrifice. The Fraternal Order of Police[111], Concerns of Police Survivors[112], the National Rifle Association[113], your state[114], and the United States Department of Justice Public Safety Officer Benefit Program[115] all provide benefits for line of duty deaths. However, those programs and outpourings of support will not make it easier for you to get through the funeral for a friend.

> *It's part of who I am. No matter what anybody else says, it's part of who I have become. It's part of my daily life. I think about it every single day. I have a lot of guilt to some of the things that I did or didn't do. Monday morning quarter backing and everybody tries to say, "Oh you know you did okay, you did it." It's not something that I process. I already know what I did or what I didn't do. It's just part of who I am. I wear this on my bracelet. It's got the initials of the two officers who were killed and the date. I think about it every day.*

Q: What was the date?
A: It was July 23, 1999.

–Name withheld

---

[111] www.grandlodgefop.org
[112] www.nationalcops.org
[113] www.nrahq.org/law/lebenefits.asp
[114] www.odmp.org/benefits
[115] www.ojp.usdoj.gov/BJA/grant/psob/psob_main.html

At its most simple explanation, the funeral in these circumstances is so devastating because you are connected to the deceased on so many levels.

While the funeral of any LEO is heartbreaking, the funeral for a fallen coworker involved in a critical incident with you will be worse. This is not *any* fallen LEO; you worked together, you ate together, and you knew each other. You will be sad and angry at the same time. You will also likely face "Survivor Syndrome," asking yourself, "Why did I live?" Add to this the fact that you may be asked to speak at the funeral, while you are still going through the investigations and your own struggle with the incident and have quite a heavy load on your heart and shoulders. These emotions and thoughts create a clear need for professional help. You should not expect to be able to get through this type of emotional trauma on your own.

As traumatic as a funeral for a fallen LEO is, the trauma for a seriously injured LEO can be worse, as their suffering, and the suffering of their family, friends, and agency never ends. LEOs injured on the street go from being in total control of their own lives to being completely dependent upon strangers for everything. Often, the agency support fades with time. The requirement that the agency provide more than medical treatment under the state's workers compensation program may be the only support that exists. Injured LEOs may be forced to medically retire on a limited or non-existent disability income at a time when they are in need of special housing and other accommodations. While LEOs can and should purchase disability insurance, and there are financial assistance programs available, the most critical type of support is the personal connection with the LEOs in your agency.

Many times, the personal support fades with time. This is not unique to LEOs. An injured coworker is out of sight and often out of mind. However, I believe from what I have seen that the problem is worse with LEOs. Perhaps it is because the injured LEO reminds us all that there is a price to pay for standing for what is right, defending those who are helpless, and placing yourself in harm's way. That cost is high.

The aftermath of a critical incident can last a long time. For LEOs injured in the line of duty, their lives may never be the same. I have met and represented LEOs who lost limbs, suffered devastating internal injuries, and lived with the effects of those injuries every day. For those LEOs, their recovery begins anew each day when the sun rises.

In 2010, a group of LEOs in Missouri started a group to help disabled LEOs in a very positive and meaningful way. Hunting For Heroes[116] is a not for profit organization that takes disabled LEOs hunting and fishing. I have the honor of serving on the Executive Board of Hunting for Heroes, aka "H4H." Founded by Chris Allen, H4H does whatever it takes and employs whatever resources are required to get wounded heroes back out in the woods or on the water. The positive impact on the injured LEOs and their families is immeasurable.

H4H makes whatever accommodations are necessary, including adaptive devices for firearms, specialized mobility devices like track wheelchairs, and any other devices required for success. These hunts take place at

---

[116] www.huntingforheroes.org

locations that allow the LEO, their spouse, and their family to get away from the stress. The LEO is able to get out into the woods and fields again and feel the autonomy and freedom they felt every day before their injury. I am proud to work with and for this wonderful organization as a Board Member. For a LEO who loves the outdoors, Hunting For Heroes can make the difference between healing and a recovery.

I have spent time with many LEOs who never returned to duty following a critical incident. Law enforcement is still in their hearts, but is no longer a part of their lives. This causes tremendous stress on a daily basis that never goes away. When a LEO loses his profession, he loses part of his purpose in life. Long after the wounds turn to scars, the injury of losing the ability to serve continues to ache. We must look for opportunities to be there to support these LEOs long after they retire from our departments. We owe it to them to take care of our own.

It's OK to Move On

I am a firm believer that LEOs have a special, short line in heaven. We serve for the right reasons, although those reasons differ depending upon whom you ask. I also believe that LEOs would want their friends and families to move beyond the pain and sorrow of their loss. As stated above, this is a process that can be quite long. Like anything we do, we must be committed to the end result. You will never forget the fallen or injured, but it is okay to continue with your life and your chosen profession.

That's the worst part about it, knowing that you did have to end somebody's life. But then again, you take the other side and say, 'I didn't ask him to do this.' That was his choice. You know, he shot me, he shot my partner. He jumped on top of me, bashed me over the head with my flashlight to get my gun, and he was more than willing to shoot me with my gun again. I'm sorry he made those decisions, but I'm happy I came out on top.

–Name withheld

Many factors affect this process. Not the least of which is the ability of the media to remind us of the old wounds. Further, civil litigation takes years to resolve. Worse still is the pace of the criminal justice system. It can take decades to bring a killer to justice through the death penalty. Sometimes, it is worse when the killer will live the rest of his life in prison. In short, the reminders of the most terrifying seconds in your life will be all around you. You must learn to keep your eyes on the horizon and stay focused on your personal mission of public service.

One of the unspoken obstacles to healing can be a loss of standing or criticism within your agency. I know of more than one situation in which the heroes who neutralized a threat were criticized for their tactics. No manual provides a tactic for every situation, nor is there any guarantee that the tactics you are taught will work. However, there are mistakes made in our profession and sometimes those mistakes have tragic consequences. We must acknowledge that we all make mistakes, but most of us are lucky enough to avoid injury to ourselves or others. It is also critical to recognize that the LEO who makes a mistake that leads to the loss or injury to another LEO is well aware of what happened. That person will hand out more punishment to himself than anyone else could give. Use the mistake for training to prevent another tragedy, but remember that when the agency turns on a LEO, she may be a step away from losing the most important and only support network available. If that occurs, the results can be tragic. We must get past the anger and disappointment we feel toward that LEO who made a critical error. There is too much at stake.

The Deadly Threat From Within – Suicide

Sometimes, we lose a LEO after the event, when the burdens of life going forward become too much for her to bear. Suicide among LEOs is a topic few trainers will discuss with the type of frank and honest language needed to address the problem. I am fortunate to have heard two such trainers at a seminar sponsored by Concerns of Police Survivors and entitled, "Traumas in Law Enforcement." You can learn more at www.nationalcops.org. The two instructors were, in order of appearance, Jack Harris and Robert E. Douglas, Jr. Both are retired LEOs with a tremendous amount of experience both as LEOs and trainers. Their dedication to their fellow LEOs and survivors is inspiring. You can learn more about Jack Harris at www.jackharris.org and Robert E. Douglas, Jr. at www.psf.org.

If you assemble 100 mental health professionals and ask them to state the root cause of suicide, you will likely receive nearly 100 different answers. However, nearly all will state that a person who intends to commit suicide will telegraph their intent in the overwhelming number of cases.

Millions of dollars and research hours have been spent to discover why people commit suicide and how to prevent such tragic deaths. Perhaps the difficulty in this research is the number of unanswered questions following every suicide. Also compounding the search for answers is a recognition that our culture does not know how to respond to a suicide. This is especially true when a LEO ends his own life.

When I was a young patrol officer, one of the officers on my shift sat down in the squad room with a black band around his badge. When a sergeant learned that the officer placed the black band in remembrance of a LEO from another jurisdiction who committed suicide on duty, the sergeant politely instructed him to remove the black band. I look back on that exchange with regret. I regret that the sergeant did not have the empathy to recognize that a suicide on duty is a tragedy for an agency and very likely related to the deceased LEO's job. I regret that the officer on my shift removed the black band. Finally, I regret that I did not understand enough about suicide among LEOs to say something in defense of my coworker.

This book is not about suicide among LEOs. There are excellent sources of information about that topic. However, I cannot adequately discuss critical incidents without briefly addressing suicide. I will never again remain silent regarding suicide among LEOs as I did on that night so long ago.

While suicide is a complex issue, we can simplify the root causes for our purposes. In short, the underlying reasons are not at issue in our analysis. A LEO may commit suicide due to marital stress, the loss of a loved one, the potential loss of a job, or many other stressors. However, for our purposes, we must recognize that any critical incident, alone or in combination with pre-existing stressors, could provide the catalyst for a suicide attempt.

For the LEO who uses deadly force, there can be tremendous guilt about the taking of a life. Most LEOs I know do not believe they will suffer a great deal of guilt. However, consider that the person you may be forced to shoot is someone's family member. They could be a juvenile, a frail elderly person, or an emotionally disturbed person. Consider also that in many situations, people will second guess your decision to shoot. Finally, what if your decision to shoot was incorrect? There are enough sources of guilt to go around.

Further consider the intense emotions surrounding an OIS, the lack of sleep, and the changes to your routine and way of life. LEOs are routinely put on five or ten days of administrative leave following an OIS. This can begin a period of isolation, from friends who no longer see you every day and coworkers reluctant to speak to you for fear of saying the wrong thing or violating agency policy.

You may also experience financial stress from an OIS. As I mentioned earlier, your agency will likely prevent you from working part-time jobs while you are on administrative leave, and possibly for a period of time after you return to duty. You may also lose overtime pay from special details, or court pay that you have come to depend upon to run your home. One solution is to prepare for this and other financial setbacks by getting your financial house in order. I highly recommend Dave Ramsey's books and programs to take you to the world of financial independence.

Finally, it is rare that an OIS involves only one LEO. Back up units also experience many of the same stressors as the LEO who uses deadly force. This is compounded when a LEO is injured or killed during the incident. The stress of the incident, followed shortly thereafter by the stress of a funeral, can prove too much for some. Some LEOs experience a tremendous amount of stress because they were out sick or on vacation when a LEO was injured or killed. The effects of stress know no boundaries and reach farther than most believe possible.

Usually, suicide is a slow, silent killer. The idea can form in an instant and grow stronger with time. Published reports[117] make it clear that suicide among LEOs can take place years after a critical incident. Only through education can we make a difference and prevent the tragedy that haunts agencies and families for generations.

While there are many signs that may warn of a possible suicide attempt, below are five signs to watch for that should encourage intervention and provoke action, sometimes as simple as asking the question, "Are you thinking about hurting yourself or taking your own life?"

Five Signs that should concern you:

1. Has the person discussed suicide?
2. Has the person begun to give away prized possessions?
3. Has the person become withdrawn from friends and family?
4. Has the person begun to abuse drugs and/or alcohol?

---

[117] Suicide Rates for 2010: General public 11/100,000; Police: 17/100,000; Army 20/100,000 Source: http://badgeoflife.com/suicides.php

5. Has the person shown signs of increased stress, lack of sleep, or loss of interest in his personal appearance?

No one ever said this was easy. In hostage negotiation school, we learned that a small number of people who intend to commit suicide probably cannot be stopped. Remember the following as you try to get help for a fellow LEO. First, your efforts may not be successful and that may have nothing to do with your sincerity or determination. Second, use common sense and be safe. Your efforts to intervene do not have to be planned, complex, or well thought out. Just do something. Just speak with the person or tell someone that you are concerned. During the editing process of this book, I attended the first funeral in my life for a friend who took his own life. I left the service with more questions than I imagined. The loss of one more LEO to suicide is one too many.

If a journey of a thousand miles begins with a single step, moving forward after a critical incident requires many steps and sometimes someone to carry you. You are worth the effort of the many people who stand ready and willing to get you through the most difficult times. Stand strong because you do not stand alone.

CHAPTER ELEVEN
MILES TO GO

"Stopping by Woods on a Snowy Evening"

Whose woods these are I think I know
His house is in the village, though;
He will not see me stopping here
To watch his woods fill up with snow

My little horse must think it queer
To stop without a farmhouse near
Between the woods and frozen lake
The darkest evening of the year.

He gives his harness bells a shake
To ask if there's some mistake.
The only other sound's the sweep
Of easy wind and downy flake.

The woods are lovely, dark and deep,
But I have promises to keep,
And miles to go before I sleep,
And miles to go before I sleep.

–Robert Frost from *New Hampshire (1923)*

In 2011, 170 LEOs lost their lives during the performance of their duties[118]. Keep in mind this number may be low due to underreporting or misclassification of suicides. I am honored and proud to represent LEOs and their families when the injuries and deaths occur under circumstances that raise a question as to whether the injury or death took place in the performance of their duties.

Each year, the Department of Justice publishes the Summary of Law Enforcement Officers Killed or Assaulted. The statistics break down these tragedies into definable categories for purposes of training, policy decisions, and clarity. The reports can be found online at www.fbi.gov. The numbers are staggering. However, the injuries and deaths are, in many instances, preventable. Wear your seatbelts! Wear your body armor! These statistics make it clear that critical incidents, injuries, and deaths among LEOs may soon reach your agency. Be ready.

As I write this chapter, my thoughts are with the Bexar County Sheriff's Office and the family and friends of Sergeant Kenneth Vann. Sergeant Vann was murdered in the early morning hours of May 28, 2011 as he sat at a red light in his patrol car. The streets are more violent for LEOs today. While the law surrounding the use of deadly force has not changed, the perception of any reasonable LEO *has* changed. LEOs have less time to react today than they did in the past, and the likelihood that a person would actually try to kill a LEO has increased exponentially in the past few years. The situation will not get any better as counties and states close budget shortfalls with early release programs. California, Kentucky, Virginia, Connecticut, Alabama, Arizona, and other states have

---

[118] Officer Down Memorial Page www.odmp.com

discussed or implemented such measures in the past two years. I hope that the media professionals will include these facts in their reports.

The proliferation of social media, cell phone video, in-car video, and surveillance cameras means that your actions will be under intense scrutiny at all times. However, you must act in accordance with the law, with a mindset of survival every time to ensure that you return home at the end of every shift.

No matter how mean the streets become or how dangerous the job becomes, LEOs will put on their badges of office and perform their sworn duties every day. For that, we are all grateful and our society is a better place.

Popeye was famous for saying, "That's all I can stand, 'cause I can't stand no more!" That's about where I am right now. I can, from memory, think about shootings that resulted in the murders of a dozen LEOs in a twenty-four month period. If I searched on the internet, I could name the incidents.

Every time it happens, police administrators, politicians, and newscasters start screaming for gun control to stop the violence against LEOs. It is a common call to action, sounds good on the news, and represents the most misguided waste of resources in history.

My challenge here is to avoid writing a long chapter. I would love to, but that would mask the simplicity of the solution to this problem. So, for all the politicians, "policy experts," and others who sit behind a desk all day, here is the simple solution. *When a person manifests an intent to violate the laws of our states and our country, especially through acts of violence, remove them from society.* There is no amount of gun control that will prove more effective, and pro-gun ownership statutes have undeniably led to a decrease in violent crime. Behind these statistics are thousands of private citizens who are alive because they used a legally owned firearm to protect themselves and their families. A wise man one said, "An armed society is a polite society[119]."

My next thought is directed to LEOs who embrace gun control laws. The very individuals and groups who seek to keep private citizens from owning and carrying firearms do not believe LEOs should possess firearms, either. There is one defined group in our country that can be disarmed quickly with the stroke of a legislator's pen: law enforcement. Think it can't happen? Look at LEOs in Europe.

Ask a gun control advocate or politician why we cannot keep criminals out of our free society and you will hear, at the root of their argument, that the cost is too high. Keeping our society and citizenry free from the oppressive effects of crime is the constitutional obligation of government. As to the cost, I have attended enough LEO funerals to know the costs. It is cheaper to keep criminals in prison.

I have read many stories of LEOs attacked simply because they were wearing the uniform. On January 23, 2011, a gunman entered a Detroit police station and shot four LEOs. The suspect was shot and killed and all of the LEOs will survive. The surveillance footage of the shooting is horrific. On November 29, 2009, four Lakewood, Washington Police Officers were not as fortunate. Maurice Clemmons assassinated four LEOs who were sitting together in a coffee shop. However we choose to categorize

---

[119] Robert A. Heinlein

these killers, or their motivation, the idea that LEOs are targeted for violent attacks is nothing new to those who wear a badge. Neither is the idea that these violent individuals rarely decide to perpetrate a violent attack as their first foray into the world of criminal acts. This was certainly the case with the late Maurice Clemmons, the killer in Lakewood, Washington, and Gregory Favors, the convicted felon who shot and killed Georgia State Trooper Chadwick LeCroy in December 2010.

At the end of 2009, there were more than 1.6 million inmates in state and federal prisons. With the current budget problems of several states, politicians are talking about releasing more inmates through early release. When will they learn? Enough about gun laws, suits against gun manufacturers, and "mean-spirited" political rhetoric. Criminals assault LEOs every day. It only makes the news when they use a firearm or take a life.

As LEOs, we have a tremendous opportunity to focus the debate. We also have an obligation to do our best to prevent future tragedies. Recently, I took a lead in the political process, and I encourage you to do the same.

I proposed a bill that would prevent any person who causes an injury to a LEO from receiving First Offender Status under Georgia law. This will prevent lenient sentences and also prevent these individuals from hiding behind a law intended to allow people to have a fresh start when they plead guilty. Assaulting a LEO has become an acceptable offense in our society. The time has come for that philosophy to end. In our country, a LEO is the highest level of authority a criminal will face. An assault on a LEO is an assault on all of us and a clear manifestation that the criminal will not respect any other law. On April 16, 2012, I stood with Senator Lindsey

Tippins, Carlton Stallings, the President of the Georgia Fraternal Order of Police, my wife Barbara and retired LEO Joy Surratt, whose injury inspired this bill, when Governor Deal signed the legislation into law. It was a proud moment for me, my firm, and the Fraternal Order of Police.

I am not the only person working to make a difference. A local LEO, Eric Smith, is working to prevent another tragedy like we experienced with the murder of Georgia Trooper Chad LeCroy on December 27, 2011. He drafted a petition that seeks to prevent the release of criminals on probation when they are arrested. What can you do in your state?

Contact your legislators. Work with them to plug the holes that allow violent criminals to walk the streets. Do not take "no" for an answer. No one knows more about the effects of violent crime than the LEOs on the street. The First Amendment gives you a voice. Use it and do not let anyone keep you silent. Join groups like the Fraternal Order of Police and the National Rifle Association who continue working hard to keep violent criminals behind bars.

I worked on the street, in training, and in investigations. I have been involved in training LEOs for more than twenty years. I was also a public relations and community outreach officer for my agency. Second only to the injury or death of a LEO, one of the biggest tragedies of these vicious attacks is the potential for all LEOs to develop a distrust for the public we serve. There is a difference between sitting with your back to the wall in a restaurant and living in fear of everyone. In a time when our communities see LEOs as heroes and role models, we cannot afford to create any distance from the public. When a thief takes property, the victim loses. If we allow violent criminals to take away the bond with our communities, we will all lose.

About seven years after I started working as a LEO, I was summoned to jury duty. The questionnaire I received required me to disclose, under oath, if I was ever a victim of a crime and to list those crimes. I thought for a minute, checked the box for "yes," and started writing. As part of my constant efforts to be accommodating, I listed the number of "counts" next to each statute. As you may imagine, there were several counts of simple assault and simple battery, more than one count of terroristic threats, a couple of counts of "solicitation of sodomy" based upon requests by several angry suspects (all of which I declined), and at least one count of aggravated assault. When we handed our forms to the jury coordinator, she read the list of crimes and said, "Wow! That's a lot." I knew at the time that my list was nowhere near as long as other LEOs I knew. LEOs see and experience a different side of our society and it is all "part of the job."

Every couple of weeks, I receive a call or email from a LEO who is concerned about the disposition of criminal charges against a particular suspect. While many of those calls involve the LEO's attempt to protect children or a particularly vulnerable victim, many others involve crimes committed against the LEO in the performance of his duties. I am always disappointed to hear how many LEOs are concerned that the prosecutors will allow a suspect to plea to lesser charges when the assault or injury occurs to a LEO. However, I understand their concerns because I have seen it happen.

There are several ways that you can prevent a suspect from getting a light plea deal when that suspect commits a crime against you. First, develop a good relationship with the prosecutors in your jurisdiction. The overwhelming majority of prosecutors support you and want to learn more about your job. Second, make certain that your report clearly outlines the details of any crime committed against you. It is not enough to say that the suspect struck you. Add that the suspect struck you in the upper chest just to the left of your badge or kicked your upper leg leaving a mark on your uniform pants. Third, you need to learn to be a victim.

Victims have some rights. As a victim, you have the right to contact the prosecutor, meet with the prosecutor, and give your input as to the charges. You also have the right to know the status of the prosecution and any deals that will be discussed with the defendant or his counsel. While the prosecutor generally has the discretion to offer and accept plea deals, you have the right to make your views known. Finally, you have the right to attend the plea proceeding. You will find that most judges want to hear from any victim who cares enough to come to the courthouse at the time of the plea.

By letting the prosecutor know that you are interested in the case and by providing photographs, invoices for damaged personal or agency equipment, and medical records documenting your injuries, you help the prosecutor learn more about the case. You also help personalize your case. Most prosecutors are swamped with case files. Make it easy for them to learn the facts about your case. If you meet a prosecutor who is not willing to listen, remember that the elected official at the top of that chain of command will listen.

There are many resources available for LEOs injured in the line of duty. I know because I am one of those resources. I have represented LEOs in civil cases against DUI drivers, people who defamed them and filed false charges against them, people who have stabbed them, and the estate of a man who shot a LEO before turning the gun on himself. I get fired up about these cases. My staff and I work hard for the LEOs we represent. This commitment is more than just a requirement for a lawyer. I believe it began my first night on the street when my first training officer, Tim Jennings, said to me, "We have to look out for each other, because there is no one else out here doing it."

In our society, we rely on law enforcement to protect us. When a suspect assaults, attacks, or injures a LEO, he or she has just faced the highest level of force our constitution will allow us to use to stop crime. The actions of that suspect should be treated differently. In an age of hate crimes legislation, I can easily make the argument that a crime against a LEO is a hate crime with implications that the malice is directed toward society as a whole. However, that would make too much sense and, as such, confuse too many who see assaults as "part of the job" for a LEO.

One final thought—beware of the individual or group who claims to have the magic solution to stop violent assaults upon LEOs. You should also recognize that you must be prepared to protect yourself, your family, and your fellow LEOs by being armed. Think about it. The following passage is a blog post from www.bluelinelawyer.com on the topic.

> *What a sad, horrifying, and bizarre way to begin 2012. From a media standpoint, there has been a lot of news to cover. A young mother shot and killed an intruder in Oklahoma; LEOs in*

Brownsville, Texas responded to a report of an armed suspect in a school on lockdown and shot the suspect; and three LEOs were murdered. Through all the commentary, there is a theme: Protecting our children.

The teen mom is being praised for being brave, and she was brave. Let's be honest, though. A lot of people in her situation are brave...and deceased. Like many private citizens, she was the victim of a crime and facing an armed attacker. She called 911 to ask for help like millions of other citizens. Fortunately, she still had a right to possess, access, and use a firearm to protect herself and her child. While much is being stated in the media about this brave mother who acted to protect her child, would her actions have been less brave if she was an eighty year old widow who lived alone? The media was attracted to this story because of the infant. You can read thousands of such stories at the Armed Citizen page of the NRA website. They have been publishing such stories for decades. However, the critical role of legal firearms ownership was lost on the media.

Ok, so I guess we know what to look for in news stories. People protecting children. Now I understand the rules. If you use deadly force to protect a child, the media and others will celebrate your efforts. Irrespective of their political opinions or beliefs, people will praise your actions. Well, not so fast...

On January 4, 2012, a school administrator in a middle school called 911 to report that a *student entered the school with a gun. First, I did say middle school. Second, this tells you that it is highly unlikely that the school had an armed LEO on the property. Parents were surprised that a child was able to get a gun into the school and "thought they had more security." The responding LEOs formed a team and entered the school that was on lockdown when they arrived. Yes, I said lockdown. The audio from the numerous cellphone calls and recordings is becoming available and it appears there is no dispute that the LEOs ordered the student to drop the weapon numerous times. Then they fired three times. They hit the suspect three times and he died. When it was released that the weapon the student **pointed at the officers** was a pellet gun, the controversy started.*

No other students were injured; none. No officers were injured; none. The only person who was injured was the person who violated state law and numerous regulations and brought a weapon to a school. This only took place after he refused to drop the weapon and pointed it at uniformed LEOs who were giving loud verbal commands while pointing firearms at him. As the chief in charge of the jurisdiction stated, "He pointed the weapon at the officers, at which point the officers that were actively engaged by the suspect fired at least twice." Kudos to the agency for holding a press conference and showing a picture of the gun. However, within twenty-four hours, the second-guessing and criticism began.

*The news outlets are carrying stories of people demanding to know why the LEOs shot the suspect three times. The parents are claiming the LEOs used excessive force, the media is demanding to know why the pellet gun was not marked with a red tip, and other the news stories are **blaming the pellet gun**! The link in the last sentence will take you to a news story with a subheading announcing, "Air pistol that looks like real gun costs teen his life." The LEOs acted not only in self-defense but entered the building to protect **700 children**, teachers, and staff. Why is the notion that they used excessive force being entertained at all? So, now I'm confused. Clearly, it is not about the children.*

Time and time again, we've seen LEOs criticized for using excessive force when they shoot a person who refuses to drop or points a "non-firearm" at LEOs. Keep in mind that a pellet gun can and will cause a serious injury or death at close range, especially to a child in a middle school. Remember also that the mother in Oklahoma shot an intruder who was armed with a knife! The reason for this insanity, I believe, is a focus on the firearm as the cause of crime and the "evil" to be remedied. Think about it, if the weapon held and pointed by the suspect in Brownsville was a firearm, little if any controversy would have seen the light of day. While you would have the routine clamor from the voice of collective ignorance that believe LEOs should never use deadly force, such stories would have been short-lived.

To prove my point, let's look at the deaths of LEOs so far this year. Agent Jared Francom with the Ogden PD in Utah was killed while serving a search warrant. Park Ranger Margaret Anderson was shot and killed while attempting to stop a fleeing suspect near the Longmire Ranger Station in Mount Rainier National Park. The killer was a suspect in the shooting of four people just prior to Ranger Anderson's death. In Puerto Rico, Sergeant Abimael Castro-Berrocales was shot and killed after stopping a speeding vehicle. In each case, there is a media firestorm about the ownership and use of firearms. I will not link to those websites or pages because I do not want to be associated with them, including one that blames Ranger Anderson's death on a recent change in the law that allows private citizens to carry firearms in parks. Never mind the fact that the suspect fortunately died before he was able to kidnap or attack any other park visitors.

When law enforcement efforts and public policy focus on the "evil" of firearms, there is a cost. Stay-at-home moms are not able to protect their children. Schools do not have armed resource officers on campus and suspects are more likely to bring weapons to a school. Money and resources that should be spent on salaries and equipment are wasted on programs to "end gun violence" and "reduce gun crimes." The pinnacle of this misdirected effort is the now infamous "Fast and Furious" program that led to the death of Border Patrol Agent Brian Terry.

You can read my comments about this program at www.bluelinelawyer.com. Make no mistake, the groups that want to disarm the public want to disarm LEOs, as well. They are the same groups that believe you should not use deadly force.

So what is the takeaway? What should LEOs make of all this coverage? Well, I believe I was right at the outset. It is all about protecting our children. The children of citizens who call for help, the school kids locked down and hiding under their desks, and, perhaps most important, the children of the LEOs in our country. Ranger Anderson's children will never again hug their mother. Those children lost something that cannot be replaced. That is why I am so passionate about convincing LEOs not to be hesitant. From all accounts, Ranger Anderson, Agent Francom, and Sergeant Castro-Berrocales did not have a chance to defend themselves and that is an all too common thread in recent shootings of LEOs. Do not let a single news story cause you to hesitate to use the appropriate level of force. The world will have years to debate your actions. You have the rest of your life to make up your mind.

In Graham v. Connor[120]*, Justice Rhenquist wrote, "The 'reasonableness' of a particular use of force must be judged from the perspective of a reasonable officer on the scene, rather than with the 20/20 vision of hindsight" and "[t]he*

---

[120] *Graham v. Connor*, 490 U.S. 386 (1989)

calculus of reasonableness must embody allowance for the fact that police officers are often forced to make split-second judgments—in circumstances that are tense, uncertain, and rapidly evolving—about the amount of force that is necessary in a particular situation." So, while you can expect second-guessing by the grossly uninformed, you can find some comfort that the USSC still recognizes the realities of law enforcement. The Court also recognizes your right to own firearms and protect yourself, as a citizen and *a LEO. Work hard to protect that right on both fronts as your life and the lives of your spouse and children may one day depend upon it. Stay safe.*

EPILOGUE

"The Road Not Taken"

Two roads diverged in a wood, and I—
I took the one less traveled by,
And that has made all the difference...

–Robert Frost from *Mountain Interval* (1916)

Taking Care of Business and the Ones You Love

If you've ever sat in one of my classes, you know that I always speak to LEOs about writing a will. I raise this issue no matter what class I am teaching because the topic is too important. I also tell my classes that I do not draft wills. I have a group of lawyers who help the LEOs I send to them.

I often hear LEOs say that they do not have any money, so they do not need a will. I could not disagree more. First, if you are killed in the line of duty, your survivors will receive a considerable amount of money from several sources. Second, a will is your opportunity to give guidance to those who survive you. If you have ever lost someone close to you, you know that a will can be a comfort to your loved ones.

Your estate consists of all of the things you own at the time of your death. If you do not have a will, your estate will be handled according to state law. Your property will be divided and a court will appoint someone to manage that process. The person who manages your estate also has the ability to bring suits on behalf of your estate. That means if someone is responsible for your death, your estate has the right to bring a suit against them. This could be an individual, a motorist, or a company regarding some sort of product liability.

When you draft a will, you should also consider guardianship for your minor children, and an advanced directive or similar document that allows someone to make medical decisions on your behalf. Finally, you can set up one or more trusts for your children. If you think there will not be any money to fund those trusts, think again.

A line of duty death has the potential to bring compensation from several sources. Most agencies provide a death benefit and most FOP lodges do the same, along with the Grand Lodge of the Fraternal Order of Police. If you are an NRA member, there is a $25,000 benefit and other funds available for scholarships for the dependents of fallen LEOs. The United States Department of Justice also has benefit programs for line of duty deaths and severe disabilities, and many states have similar programs. *Concerns of Police Survivors* has a list of resources available to survivors.

You can write your own will, but it is selfish to do so. This is a technical area of law and the mistakes you make will only burden those who survive you. Even though I am an attorney, I hired a lawyer to draft wills for my wife and me because it was too important and I do not write wills every day. I'm certain that there are lawyers in your area willing to provide reduced will-related services for LEOs in your community. All you need to do is ask.

Make certain a trusted friend or two have a copy of the will to make things easier and let other friends and relatives know where they can find a copy. Your survivors will have a lot on their shoulders. These small steps will help them.

I know you feel the same way about needing a will as I do in one respect. The Grim Reaper better not bring a sickle to a gunfight, 'cause I am not going anywhere without a fight! However, there is no denying that we will all leave this earth at some time. Far from being a way to divide a fortune, a will helps your survivors through the most devastating time in their lives.

Professionalism in Extreme Circumstances

I am continually proud to represent LEOs who demonstrate their commitment to the highest ideals of professionalism on a daily basis. The following blog post from www.bluelinelawyer.com discusses a topic that is sensitive, controversial, and important for LEOs. It involves the extraordinary efforts of LEOs to arrest and prosecute cop killers. The title of the post is, "Cop Killer Wanted: Alive, if possible."

> *Now I know my use of the term "cop killer" will no doubt have someone jumping up and down. However, in an age of dashcam videos, the prevalence of surveillance video, and handheld video capability on cellphones, we are seeing a trend. Many shootings of LEOs are memorialized on video. The value of these videos is immeasurable to prosecution and training. For my purposes, based upon my beliefs and analysis, if a perpetrator is caught on video shooting a LEO, I will call him or her a cop killer. The camera does not lie.*
>
> *With the increase of LEOs killed in violent attacks this year and last, many have asked why LEOs go to such extraordinary lengths to take cop killers into custody? In many instances, LEOs negotiate cop killers into surrendering when the perpetrator actually* wants *a violent confrontation. I thought this question deserved some contemplation especially for the civilian readers of this blog.*

I did a little research and confirmed what I suspected: nearly every LEO oath of office includes a solemn oath to uphold the Constitution of the United States. But what does that mean in practice? Well, it is more than avoiding unreasonable searches and seizures. This portion of the LEO's oath of office means that we guarantee due process to every person accused of any crime. Due process includes the obligation to affect every arrest using the least amount of force necessary. It also means affording the accused the benefit of the protections of our Constitution, including counsel, a speedy and public trial, and the right to confront witnesses against him, to name but a few.

So why are so many cop killers taken into custody? The short answer is because many brave men and women risk their lives and bring to bear every resource to do so. The longer answer is that these efforts and resources are focused upon a principle that our LEO oath is more than a piece of paper we sign. It is a commitment to carry out the obligation that we voluntarily accepted: to uphold the Constitution of the United States. Like the use of force in every context, LEOs react to the level of force facing them. With so many perpetrators, LEOs across our country do everything possible to use the least amount of force necessary to perform their duties.

Take one look at the Officer Down Memorial Page at www.odmp.org and you will see that violent attacks on LEOs are increasing at an alarming rate. Readers of this blog will know my theory as to why: stop letting violent criminals out of prison! However, for every LEO killed in the line of duty, there was a group of LEOs who were willing to do everything possible to put their duty first and effect an arrest of the suspect.

The next time you hear or read about someone complaining how LEOs violate people's rights, you can stand proud and respond that when pushed to the limit of human emotion, LEOs consistently uphold the Constitution and arrest those who assault and kill LEOs. Put this scenario before our critics, "You learn that your best friend is dead simply because he did his job. You have access to a firearm and control over media access at the location of the person who killed him. You know that your friend's children will never see their parent again. You also know that the criminal justice system will move slowly to prosecute and punish the perpetrator. Would you have the courage and integrity to put your life in danger to provide the killer his day in court?" All across the United States, LEOs do so in every instance. Honor is doing what you must rather than what you desire.

Because LEOs uphold their oaths, because they risk their lives to guarantee constitutional protection to strangers, because they exercise discretion and commitment to duty before self every day, I will keep working to protect their due process rights. To the warriors who pursue

cop killers, I say, "Thank you for making us all
proud." When you meet those fallen officers
again in heaven, they will join God in praising
you. "Blessed are the peacemakers; for they shall
be called the children of God" (Matthew 5:9).

Long before furloughs of LEOs and budget cutbacks in
the face of increasing attacks on LEOs, Desiderius Erasmus
famously said, "In the land of the blind, the one-eyed man
is king." Now I never met Mr. Erasmus, but I am pretty
certain that during his lifetime there was little discussion
of laying off LEOs, sending LEOs home several hours
before the end of their shift to save overtime, and
disbanding specialized units to supplement patrol
functions. However, from what I have seen, his quote is
spot-on and provides a clear path for all of us who wear
the badge or support those who do.

Violent attacks on LEOs are not a new phenomenon.
The Northlake Bank robbery in 1967, Norco Bank robbery
in 1980, and the active shooter who murdered four
Lakewood Police Officers in 2009 are stark reminders that
LEOs have been and always will be under attack.
However, what is lost among the statistics of the
shootings, the politics of the response, and the speeches at
memorial services is an inescapable truth of every violent
attack on a LEO: it could have been worse. As bad as the
loss of a LEO on a traffic stop or the murder of students on
a campus will always be, each one could have been worse.
More often than not, the carnage ceased because of an
accelerated LEO response or because of pressure from the
response.

I am about as politically and fiscally conservative a
person as you will find. However, when it comes to LEOs

and all of public safety, furloughs are unacceptable. The great statesman Henry Clay once said, "Government is a trust, and the officers of the government are trustees; and both the trust and the trustees are created for the benefit of the people." Citizens are not shareholders of the government. A shareholder looks to a dividend in the form of cash. A citizen should properly look to the government to provide a safe environment within which she can live, work, and raise a family. When a government furloughs LEOs, the obligations that come with the role of a trustee dictate that such actions must be a last resort.

So the LEOs and LEO supporters who read this should be prepared to raise a flag of caution whenever public safety resources are eliminated or reduced. Have on hand the statistics that prove your point. More than quoting national crime statistics, look at local response times, calls for service, and crime reports. Meet with your government officials, attend public forums, and speak out. Your speech is protected as long as you speak on matters of public concern. The reduction in service that will result from furloughs will affect you as members of the community, and you have a right to speak up. Speak about the safety of the public not the affect on your wallet.

When you hear or read inaccurate information, counter it quickly. You will find that the public wants to be informed about the facts and they overwhelmingly value your input. You are the subject matter experts on crime, law enforcement, and officer safety. Do not allow anyone else to claim that title.

In many respects, we are living in a land of the blind. LEOs do their jobs with both eyes open and must do so to stay alive. You are the leaders in your communities. If your government officials are not going in the right direction, you can lead your citizens toward the light. They will follow your lead if you act professionally, stick to the facts, and work within our political system to make your voice heard. You may not be king, but your efforts will save lives.

Continued Support from the Courts

On Thursday, June 9, 2011, the USSC released its opinion of *Sykes v. United States*[121]. The case settles a legal question that split federal circuits: Is the attempt to flee or elude the LEOs in a vehicle a violent crime? The short answer is "Yes." You can find the opinion at www.supremecourt.gov.

The USSC examined this question in connection with a mandatory sentencing case. Put simply, Sykes claimed that fleeing from LEOs in a vehicle in Indiana was a felony, but not a violent felony. Sykes was fighting a mandatory sentencing under the federal Armed Career Criminal Act. The USSC examined the Indiana law at issue from one of Sykes' prior convictions, as well as the crime of fleeing or attempting to elude LEOs in a vehicle. In a great opinion, Justice Kennedy outlined why this crime constitutes a violent felony. I recommend that you take the time to read the opinion.

Like in all other appellate opinions, the USSC used prior case law and public policy to explain the reason behind the opinion. The Sykes opinion explains the evil behind the crime of using a vehicle to flee or attempt to elude LEOs. "The attempt to elude capture is a direct challenge to an officer's authority. It is a provocative and dangerous act that dares, and in a typical case requires, the

---

[121] ____ US____, 131 S.Ct. 2267(2011).

officer to give chase. The felon's conduct gives the officer reason to believe that the defendant has something more serious than a traffic violation to hide."

Justice Kennedy went on to cite to *Scott v. Harris*, a 2007 opinion I discussed in Chapter 7, The Civil Side of Critical Incidents in which the USSC held that LEOs were not required to abandon efforts to chase a suspect in the hope that the suspect would stop fleeing and stated, "Confrontation with police is the expected result of vehicle flight. It places property and persons at serious risk of injury[122]."

I am certain that most if not all LEOs will cheer this opinion. Suspects who flee and attempt to elude LEOs in a vehicle place both the public and the LEOs in the chase at risk. Like many other opinions from the USSC, this case should confirm for you that the USSC will read your reports, watch your videos, pay attention to your trial testimony, and maintain a practical approach to law enforcement in the United States. Keep this in mind when you start your next shift.

Future Threats to LEOs

I would like to end with a reprint of a blog post from www.bluelinelawyer.com about a dangerous trend: assaults on LEOs by armed foreign nationals.

Border Patrol Agent Brian Terry: Do you remember him?

---

[122] ____ US____, 131 S.Ct. 2267, 2274(2011).

For me, the death of a LEO in the line of duty is a tragedy. When that death is due to a violent attack, it symbolizes an affront to every principle of freedom and security that we hold dear in the United States. For in our society, LEOs represent the highest level of force and authority we are permitted to put forth against crime and in our efforts to preserve order and protect the public.

*On December 14, 2010, Border Patrol Agent Brian Terry was killed in a firefight with three foreign nationals who fired upon him and other agents knowing they were firing upon LEOs. According to reports, the three foreign nationals were "patrolling" an area of the United States known as Mesquite Seep, Arizona. Let me say that again because it appears this **fact** is lost in all of the reports in the media. Three foreign nationals were **armed** inside of the sovereign borders of our country and fired on LEOs. As I stated above, short of the deployment of the United States military, these foreign nationals were faced with the highest level of authority we are able to put forth within the restraints of our Constitution. Brian Terry and his fellow LEOs stood as a representation of our country, our government and all of us. With each pull of the trigger, the perpetrators fired not only at a group of LEOs but at everything our country stands for.*

My anger at the failure of the Fast and Furious program is not a secret. I have voiced my opinions in many forums including this blog. I have watched the congressional hearings and followed the vote to hold Attorney General Eric Holder in civil and criminal contempt of Congress. The issues contained in those hearings and that vote are topics for future blog posts. Today I write about the more pressing issue that seems to be flying under the media radar.

*We are a sovereign country. We should have a zero tolerance policy for the presence of armed foreign nationals within our borders. I have no doubt that Canadian and Mexican officials would not tolerate American citizens walking around displaying arms within their borders! In the case of Agent Terry's death, foreign nationals within our borders fired upon LEOs! They shot at them and killed Agent Terry. Where is the outrage about this in the media? As stated above, the underlying premise that guns are the problem and not the criminal activity at the border is detrimental. The misguided emphasis people are placing upon the "evils" of the firearms at issue in this case is placing LEOs at risk **every day**. Far from the safety and security of Washington, D.C., LEOs go to work every day in Arizona, Texas, New Mexico and other border states facing a real threat of assault from a foreign force. The fact that these attacks are reportedly not sanctioned by the Mexican government is little comfort to these LEOs and their families.*

It is time to push for our government to put an end to the sieve that has become our southern border. It is time to put in place a zero tolerance policy to foreign nationals entering our sovereign borders carrying weapons and committing crimes against our citizenry. The immigration crisis on our southern border is more than a news story about a court case. The United States Supreme Court was asked to rule on an Arizona law based upon a lawsuit brought by the United States Department of Justice. Perhaps the federal government should have used those resources to resolve the problem. As to the propriety of state and local LEOs being involved in enforcing our federal immigration laws, you must examine that question in a light not available to the USSC: the very safety and security of our country is at stake. Further, consider this scenario. If a foreign force landed on the shores of Georgia, would you expect state and local LEOs to do nothing? Waiting for the National Guard or other divisions of the United States military to arrive and repel the foreign invaders would not be an option.

Brian Terry and his partners stood fast for all of us. They displayed a badge of office as a line in the sand against all criminal elements. LEOs should not be forced to face attacks from armed foreign nationals. However, that has become part of the mission and daily reality of all LEOs serving near our border. Brian Terry paid with his life for a principle he believed in. In the midst of the current media frenzy, let us all remember him and his family. May God watch over all of our LEOs as they continue to do the job few in our country are willing to perform and even few farther still are willing to acknowledge. Stay safe.

There is no magic solution to crime or violent assaults on LEOs. I know that efforts to focus solely upon the instrumentalities of the assaults, mainly firearms, have failed miserably. In my humble opinion, only control of the criminals who act out and demonstrate their desire and propensities to commit violent acts on members of society will stem the tide of growing assaults on LEOs. We need to ensure our LEOs are trained and equipped to respond to the violent criminals they face. When they do encounter the worst society has to throw at them, they must be prepared to handle the criminal, administrative, and state licensing investigations that will follow.

Be Proud, Steadfast, and Prepared

Hopefully this book opened your eyes, clarified your focus, or at least made you consider the gravity of the events following any critical incident and especially an OIS. I hope you always begin each day proud to serve your country and your community as a LEO.

Devote the time necessary to learn the concepts in this book and to prepare for the day that you are forced to use deadly force. Being informed of your rights is only half the battle. You must be prepared to assert and defend those rights and have an attorney waiting in the wings to assist you.

As you stand up and voluntarily undertake the role of society's protectors, I will be there standing behind you. You may go through a long and rough journey following an OIS or critical incident, but you will not weather the storm alone.

Stay safe.

REFERENCES

Sample Garrity Warnings[1]

> ### XXXXXXXX Police Department
>
> ### Office of Professional Standards
>
> ### Internal Affairs

This GARRITY WARNING is being administered consistent with an Internal Administrative Investigation consistent with Garrity v. New Jersey, 385 U.S. 493 87 S. CT. 616 (1967) and uniform Sanitation Men Association, Inc. Et. Al., v. Commissioner of Sanitation of the City of New York, Et. Al. 392 U.S.

You are being questioned as part of an official, internal, administrative investigation which is being conducted on behalf of the City by an investigator who is a designee of the Chief of Police.

You will be asked questions specifically directed and narrowly related to the performance of your official duties and / or fitness for office. You are entitled to all of the rights and privileges guaranteed by the Constitution and Laws of the State and the Constitution of the United States of America, including the right not to be compelled to incriminate yourself.

You are advised that if you should refuse to testify or answer any questions relating to the performance of your

---

[1] These documents were provided by agencies on the condition of anonymity.

official duties and / or fitness for office, you shall be subject to departmental charges which could result in disciplinary action or termination of employment.

Neither your statements nor any information or evidence which is gained by reason of such statements can be used as evidence against you in any subsequent criminal proceeding, **(except for perjury or obstruction of justice charges).** However, these statements and any information or evidence which is gained by reason of such statements can be used against you in subsequent departmental charges.

Employee Name (print)	**Signature**	**Date**
Investigator Name (print)	**Signature**	**Date**

XXXXXXX POLICE DEPARTMENT
Garrity Advisory

To: _____

Date: _____

From:_____

Subject: Administrative Investigation of Employee Misconduct

I/A Case Number(s): _____

Allegations of employee misconduct must be taken seriously by all concerned. All complainants are warned that to knowingly give false statements may result in criminal prosecution. As an employee, you need to understand that for you to refuse to truthfully answer questions relating to the performance of your official duties and/or fitness for duty will result in disciplinary action up to, and including, termination of employment for the violations of D.O.M. Chapter 5, Section C, Standards of Conduct, #2,*Insubordination* and/or D.O.M. Chapter 5, Section C, Standards of Conduct, #25 *Internal Affairs.*

You will be asked questions specifically directed and closely related to the performance of your official duties and/or fitness for office. You do not have the right to have an attorney present during this administrative proceeding. The Internal Affairs Section will record the interview and a copy of the recording may be obtained once a disposition has been made. If an employee surreptitiously records the interview they will be subject to disciplinary action up to, and including, termination of employment for the violations of entitled D.O.M. Chapter 5, Section C, Standards of Conduct, #2 *Insubordination.* Depending on the nature of the Administrative Investigation, the Chief of Police or their designee may require you to submit to a polygraph examination, participate in a line-up, be photographed, submit financial disclosure statements, and/or submit to a medical examination. However, neither the statement(s) nor evidence you provide for this Administrative Investigation can be used against you in a criminal proceeding, except for perjury or obstruction of justice.

Above all, please remember that these investigations are designed to protect many interests, including your own. The investigations also identify problems in policies or training, the correction of which will benefit all of us.

Your cooperation in this investigation does not constitute a waiver of any appeal, grievance, or other legal right(s). Until a final disposition has been rendered, and the case formally closed, you are hereby ordered not to discuss this investigation with anyone other than personnel assigned to the Internal Affairs Unit. (This does not preclude the right of an employee to consult with an attorney or representative of his/her choice at a time other than during an administrative interview).

I have read and understand the above information.

_____

Witness   Signature

_____

Witness   Date   Time

BIBLIOGRAPHY

Administrative Investigations of Police Shootings and Other Critical Incidents: Officer Statements and Use of Force Reports Part One: Prologue. 2008. AELE Mo. L. J. 201.

American Law Institute. *The Model Penal Code American Law Institute.* Accessed October 29, 2012. www.ali.org

An Encyclopedia Britannica Company: Merriam-Webster. *Client.* Accessed October 29, 2012. http://www.merriam-webster.com/dictionary/client

Black's Law Dictionary 9th Ed. 2009.

Bureau of Justice Assistance. *Multijurisdictional Task Forces.* Accessed October 29, 2012. http://www.ojp.usdoj.gov/BJA/evaluation/program-law-enforcement/forces1.htm

City of Warrensville Heights v. Jennings, 569 N.E.2d 489, 494 (OH 1991).

Concerns of Police Survivors. *C.O.P.S: Concerns of Police Survivors.* Accessed October 29, 2012. www.nationalcops.org

Council of Superior Court Judges of Georgia. *Suggested Pattern Jury Instructions: Criminal Cases State of Georgia.* Vol. 2. 00.060.

Federal Rule of Evidence 502. 2008.

Fennell v. Gilstrap, 559 F.3d 1212 (11th Cir. 2009).

Florida National Guard and St. Petersburg College. *Multijurisdictional Counter Drug Task Force Training.* Accessed October 29, 2012. www.mctft.com

Fraternal Order of Police. *Fraternal Order of Police.* Accessed October 29, 2012. www.grandlodgefop.org

Frost, Robert. "The Road not Taken." In *Mountain Interval.* Henry Holt and Company, 1916.

GA POST Council v. Anderson, 290 Ga. App. 91, 94, 658 S.E.2d 840, 843 (2008).

Ga. Comp. R. & Regs. r. 464-3-.06.

Ga.Const. art. I, § 1, ¶ I

Garner v. Broaderick, 392 U.S. 273 (1968)

Garrity v. State of N.J., 385 U.S. 493, 479, 87 S. Ct. 616, 620, 17 L. Ed. 2d 562 (1967).

Georgia General Assembly. *Official Code of Georgia Annotated*. Title 35; 1982. Atlanta, GA.

Graham v. Conner 490 U.S. 386 (1989).

Harlow v. Fitzgerald, 457 U.S. 800 (1982)

Hood v. Carsten, 267 Ga. 579, 580, 481 S.E.2d 525, 527 (1997)

Hunting For Heroes. *H4H: Hunting for Heros*. Accessed October 29, 2012. www.huntingforheroes.org

Illinois Criminal Justice Information Authority, *On Good Authority*, Vol. 6, No. 6 "A comparison of local and multi jurisdictional drug enforcement efforts in Illinois." Feb. 2003.

Kalkines v. United States, 473 F.2d 1391 (Ct. Cl. 1973).

Lewis v. State, 243 Ga. 443, 445, 254 S.E.2d 830, 832 (1979).

Lingler v. Fechko, 312 F.3d 237, 239 (6th Cir. 2002).

Miranda v. Arizona 384 U.S. 436 (1966).

Mitsubishi Motors Credit of America, Inc. v. Robinson & Stephens, Inc., 263 Ga.App. 168, 587 S.E.2d 146 (2003).

Mixon v. City of Warner Robins. 260 Ga. 385 (1994).

Mutual Aid: Multijurisdictional Partnerships for Meeting Regional Threats. Sept. 2005 Publication No. NCJ 210679.

N.L.R.B. v. Weingarten, 420 U.S. 251 (1975).

National Rifle Association. *Law Enforcement: Benefits from the NRA*. Accessed October 29, 2012. www.nrahq.org/law/lebenefits.asp

Office of Justice Programs. *Bureau of Justice Assistance.*
Accessed October 29, 2012.
www.ojp.usdoj.gov/BJA/grant/psob/psob_main.html

Officer Down Memorial Page. Federal & State Survivor
Benefits. Accessed October 29, 2012.
www.odmp.org/benefits

Officer Down Memorial Page. *Officer Down Memorial Page.*
Accessed October 29, 2012. www.odmp.com

Probation & Corrections Peace Officers Association. *Peace
Officers Bill of Rights.* Accessed October 29, 2012.
http://www.pcpoa.org/index.php?option=com_content
&view=article&id=6&Itemid=8

*Re: Jeffrey Deal, Superior Court of Laurens County September 8,
2011,* Transcript P. 127 Lines 9-11.

S. Guar. Ins. Co. of Georgia v. Ash, 192 Ga. App. 24, 28, 383
S.E.2d 579, 583 (1989).

Scott v. Harris, 550 U.S. 372 (2007).

State Bar of Georgia. *Georgia Rules of Professional Conduct
2.1.* Accessed October 29, 2012.
http://www.gabar.org/barrules/georgia-rules-of-
professional-conduct.cfm

State v. Thompson 288 Ga. 165 (2010).

Strength v. Lovett, 311 Ga. App. 35 (2011) on Nov. 30, 2011.

Suicide Rates for 2010: General public 11/100,000; Police:
17/100,000; Army 20/100,000 Source:
http://badgeoflife.com/suicides.php

Swanson, C.R. et al, *Criminal Investigations, 6th Ed.* 1996 pp.
224 & 225.

Tennessee v. Garner 471 U.S. 1 (1985).

U.S. Constitution, Amendment XIV.

*Uniform crime report: Law Enforcement Officers Killed and
Assaulted, 2010,* 2001-2010 FBI Summary of Law
Enforcement Officers Killed or Assaulted Table 67,

prepared by the Federal Bureau of Investigation, U.S. Department of Justice (Washington DC, 2010).

Uniformed Sanitation Men Ass'n v. Comm'r of Sanitation of City of New York, 392 U.S. 280, 283-84 (1968).

Williams, Hershel Woodrow. *VHP Collection Hershel Woodrow Williams.* In the Veterans History Project Database (American Folklife Center, Library of Congress). 2003.

WHEN COPS KILL

The Aftermath of a Critical Incident

Lance J. LoRusso, Esq.

A Blue Line Lawyer publication

www.bluelinelawyer.com

About the Author

 Lance LoRusso began his law enforcement career in 1988 and has been practicing law since 1999. His practice focuses on representing law enforcement officers in all areas including responding to the scene of officer involved shootings, employment appeals, administrative and criminal investigations and state licensing inquiries. Lance also represents law enforcement officers when they are injured on and off duty. He has obtained settlements for law enforcement officers ranging from a few thousand dollars to over two million dollars. He has litigated cases on behalf of law enforcement officers facing civil, administrative and criminal charges. Lance serves as an advisor for several agencies and teaches at law enforcement academies and conferences around the State of Georgia. His articles and blog posts have been featured in LEO publications, including *SWAT,* and websites such as lawenforcementtoday.com and officerresource.com.